T0095995

# YOSEMITE
# NATIONAL
# PARK
# TRIVIA

MICHAEL ELSOHN ROSS

RIVERBEND
PUBLISHING

## DEDICATION
*To my son Nick and my wife Lisa, for tolerating my trivia-itis
through the years, especially while I was writing this book.*

## ACKNOWLEDGMENTS
*Thanks to Linda Eade, the amazing librarian at the Yosemite Research Library,
and expert ranger naturalist Erik Westerlund for their assistance.*

*Yosemite National Park Trivia*
© 2011 Michael Elsohn Ross
Published by Riverbend Publishing, Helena, Montana

ISBN 13: 978-1-60639-031-3

Printed in the United States of America.

2  3  4 5 6 7 8 9 FS 25 24 23 22

Cover design by Ron Trout
Text design by Barbara Fifer

Riverbend Publishing
P.O. Box 5833
Helena, MT 59604
riverbendpublishing.com

# Contents

# GEOGRAPHY

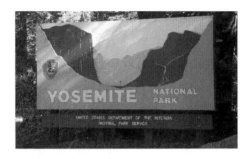

Q. Yosemite is almost the same size of which state?
1) Delaware   2) New Jersey   3) Rhode Island
A. 3) Yosemite has an area 1189 square miles, compared to Rhode Island's area of 1,545 square miles.

Q. How does Yosemite rank in size among all national parks in the USA?
1) third   2) eleventh   3) fourteenth
A. 3) Yosemite is ranked fourteenth in size. Wrangel-St. Elias, the biggest national park, is 17 times larger than Yosemite.

Q. Yosemite is larger than which of these national parks?
1) Great Smoky Mountains   2) Death Valley   3) Grand Canyon
A. 1) Yosemite is more than twice as large as Great Smoky Mountains National Park.

**Q.** The population density of the east end of Yosemite Valley on a busy summer day is greater than the population density of which two cities?
1) Los Angeles   2) Mexico City   3) San Francisco
**A.** 1) or 3) On a jam-packed summer day or holiday the number of people per square mile in the "developed" part of Yosemite Valley is greater than Los Angeles or San Francisco.

**Q.** The geographic center of Yosemite National Park is:
1) Half Dome   2) Mt. Hoffman   3) Tuolumne Meadows
**A.** 2) From the summit of Mt. Hoffman the 360° view includes most of the park. It is named after Charles F. Hoffman, cartographer and topographer for the California Geological Survey from 1860 to 1873. At the base of the peak is May Lake, named after Hoffman's wife, Lucy Mayotta.

**Q.** The highest peak in Yosemite is:
1) Mt. Hoffman   2) Cathedral Peak   3) Mt. Lyell
**A.** 3) Mt. Lyell is, at 13,114'. The second highest peak in the park is Mt. Dana at 13,053'.

**Q.** Mt. Lyell is named after:
1) a sheepherder   2) a senator   3) a British geologist
**A.** 3) The Britisher. Sir Charles Lyell's multi-volume book, *Principles of Geology*, was published in 1830 and immediately established him as the lead geologist of his day. The book's subtitle, "An attempt to explain the former changes of the Earth's surface by reference to causes now in operation," indicates his support for James Hutton's theory of uniformitarianism, a theory that led to the awareness of the Earth's vast age.

*Charles Lyell*

**Q.** What is the lowest elevation in Yosemite National Park?
**A.** At 2,127', the park boundary at El Portal is the lowest part

---

*Yosemite, at 7.5 square miles, is nearly as large as Key West off Florida (7 square miles).*

of the park. The Merced Gorge above it contains many plant and animal species common to the Sierra Nevada foothills.

Q. What is the elevation difference between the park's lowest and highest points?
1) 9,000'  2) 10,000'  3) almost 11,000'
A. 3) The 10,987' of elevation range within in the park allows for a wide range of ecological zones and plant communities from oak woodland and chaparral to arctic-alpine meadows and fell fields. In between there is a great diversity of forest and meadows communities.

Q. Which national park has the greatest elevation range between its lowest and highest point?
A. Wrangel-St. Elias. From its lowest point at sea level the park rises 18,008' to its highest point at the peak of Mt. Saint Elias, the second highest peak in the United States.

Q. What is the actual elevation of the Yosemite Valley floor?
A. The valley is 4,094' above sea level at Mirror Lake and 4,035' at Happy Isles. Curry and Yosemite villages are slightly less than 4,000' and Bridalveil Meadow is about 3,900'. Generally the elevation of Yosemite Valley is given as 4,000'. The difference in elevation between the east and west ends of the valley is almost 200'.

Q. What was the estimated elevation of Half Dome in 1856?
A. Thomas W. Long estimated it was 4,484' above the valley floor.

Q. What is the actual elevation of the summit of Half Dome above the Valley?
A. 4,796, frequently rounded off to 4,800'. The elevation of the summit of Half Dome is 8,842' above sea level.

---

*It is by far the grandest of all the special temples of Nature*
*I was ever permitted to enter. —John Muir*

Q. What other names has Half Dome had?
A. Tissiack and South Dome.

Q. Before it was known as El Capitan, this rock was known by what Ahwahneechee Indian name?
1) Tissiack   2) Pohono   3) Tutokanula
A. 3) Tu-tok-a-nu-la is the oldest known name for El Capitan.

Q. Tu-tok-a-nu-la is the name of which animal?
1) coyote   2) inchworm   3) spider
A. 2) Tu-tok-a-nu-la, the inchworm, is the hero of a legend that explains the origin of the rock.

Q. The number of lakes in Yosemite is
1) 58   2) 163   3) 265
A. 3) The majority of Yosemite's 265 lakes are above 5,000' in elevation.

Q. The largest lake in Yosemite National Park is
1) May   2) Tenaya
3) Tilden
A. 2) The largest, Tenaya, lies at the headwaters of Tenaya Creek, which flows in Yosemite Valley.

*Tenaya Lake*

Q. How many man-made lakes (reservoirs) are in the park?
1) none   2) one   3) two
A. 3) Lake Eleanor and Hetch Hetchy reservoirs are the two artificial lakes, and supply water and power to the city of San Francisco.

Q. What lake in the Yosemite Valley was created by a rockslide and has now become a meadow?
A. Mirror Lake.

Q. How many rivers originate in Yosemite National Park?
1) one   2) two   3) three   4) four

---

*The U.S. Wilderness Area designation means that mechanized and motorized activities—recreational and commercial—are banned, to protect wildlife and habitat, and offer peace to humans.*

A. 2) The Merced and Tuolumne rivers, two of the ten main rivers in the Sierra Nevada, originate in the high elevations of the park. Both rivers supply water for agriculture in California's Central Valley.

Q. How big is the drainage basin that feeds the Merced River?
1) 999 sq. miles   2) 1,726 sq. miles   3) 2,598 sq. miles
A. 2) At 1,726 square miles, this basin is as large as the country of Luxembourg.

Q. The Tuolumne River has a larger drainage basin than the Merced.
1) True   2) False
A. 2) True. The Tuolumne drainage basin is approximately 3,000 square miles, which is larger than the drainage of the Merced River as well as the state of Delaware.

Q. Which river is longer?
1) Tuolumne   2) Merced   3) They're equal.
A. 1) The Tuolumne river runs a distance of 150 miles, making it the longer. The length of the Merced is 112 miles. The width of California is 250 miles.

Q. What Yosemite mountain is a source of both the Merced and Tuolumne rivers?
1) Mt. Hoffman   2) Mt. Dana   3) Mt. Lyell
A. 3) The south side of Mt. Lyell feeds the upper Merced River and the north side is the main headwaters of the Tuolumne.

Q. Within the original Yosemite National Park boundary, which river did not have all of its headwaters protected?
A. Before boundary changes in 1905, the northern drainages of Tuolumne River were not within the park. Today, the headwaters of both the Merced and Tuolumne rivers are within park boundaries.

Q. Why is this important?
A. If the headwaters of a river are not protected they can be contaminated by activities such as logging, mining, and grazing, which can cause erosion and pollution all along the stream.

---

*Almost 95% of Yosemite National Park is a designated Wilderness Area, meaning that even bicycling is banned in that portion.*

Q. Which river flows through Hetch Hetchy Valley?
1) Merced   2) Stanislaus  3) Tuolumne
A. 3) The Tuolumne River enters Hetch Hetchy after passing through the Muir Gorge. The Merced flows through Yosemite Valley.

Q. What river is fed by both the Merced and Tuolumne rivers?
1) San Joaquin
2) Sacramento
3) Stanislaus
A. 2) The San Joaquin River drains all of the rivers of the central and southern Sierra except the Kern and Kings rivers. Besides the Merced and Tuolumne rivers, the Stanislaus River is its other major tributary.

*Merced River*

Q. Where does the water from the San Joaquin River enter the ocean?
1) Santa Cruz   2) San Francisco Bay   3) Los Angeles
A. 2) The San Joaquin River is the second biggest river in California. It joins the state's largest river, the Sacramento, in the San Joaquin Delta, and both flow into San Francisco Bay where their waters eventually mix with the Pacific Ocean.

Q. Where has water from the South Fork of the Merced been found in groundwater?
1) Mt. Diablo   2) Fresno   3) Santa Cruz Mountains
A. 3) Some of the groundwater from the South Fork percolates through rock layers under the San Joaquin Valley and ends up in the Santa Cruz Mountains.

Q. In 1984 the Tuolumne River was designated a Wild and Scenic River. How many miles of the river are protected under this designation?
A. Congress added 83 miles of the Tuolumne River to the National Wild and Scenic Rivers System. Fifty-four miles of the Tuolumne flow through Yosemite National Park.

---

*Yosemite has 68 miles of unpaved roads,*
*and 214 miles of paved ones.*

Q. In 1987 the Merced River was also designated a Wild and Scenic River. How many miles of the Merced are protected?

A. 122 miles of the main stem and South Fork of the Merced River, including the forks of Red Peak, Merced Peak, Triple Peak, and Mt. Lyell are part of the Wild and Scenic Rivers System. The National Park Service manages 81 miles of the Merced Wild and Scenic River, encompassing both the main stem and the South Fork in Yosemite National Park.

Q. How long does it take to drive from the South Entrance to Tioga Pass?
1) An hour and a half   2) two hours   3) three hours
A. 3) The route from the southeast corner of the park to the entrance on the east side can take three hours.

Q. How long would it take to drive to all road-accessible park destinations in one day?
1) five hours   2) six hours   3) more than seven hours
A. 3) It requires at least seven hours of driving time to drive to all major park destinations.

   To allow time for walks, a visit of three or more days is recommended to get an overview of the whole park. A large portion of a lifetime is recommended for anyone truly intent on experiencing most of the park locations during a variety of seasons!

Q. Which two park roads are closed in winter?
A. The Tioga Road and the Glacier Point Road from Badger Pass to Glacier Point are not plowed after the first big snows in

November. Both roads usually open in May. The latest opening date for the Tioga Road was July 10, 1933. The shortest time period that it was open was 69 days in 1944, and the longest was 263 days during the drought of 1976-77. The average number of open days is 156.

*Tioga Pass*

---

*Following trails or old-fashioned cross-country hiking are the ways to see most of Yosemite.*

### Name Game

Q. What park feature has an Iroquois Indian name?
A. Tioga Pass was named by miners from Iroquois territory in New York State. At 9,945 feet it is the loftiest highway pass in California.

Q. What park meadow was named after a stagecoach driver?
A. Monroe Meadows was named in honor of George Monroe, a black stagecoach driver and guide, who worked for the Washburn brothers from 1868 to 1886.

Q. What park peak is named after a cook who worked for the United States Geological Survey for twenty years?
A. In 1916, Stephen T. Mather, the first director of the new National Park Service, organized a camping trip in the Sierra Nevada for influential journalists and policy makers from Congress, as well as the scientific and business communities. He wanted it to be a trip they would remember. He showed them some of the most spectacular scenery in the Sierra as they camped in luxury. Mather borrowed Tie Sing, a well respected Chinese trail cook, from the Geological Survey. Each day Sing prepared a rich backcountry meal served on freshly built log tables set with linen table cloths. After twenty years of cooking for the geological survey, Tie died from an accident while in the field.

Q. Which Yosemite geographic features are named after John Muir?

*Muir Glacier in Alaska's Glacier Bay National Park honors John Muir, who visited that state many times.*

A. The Muir Gorge on the Tuolumne River is the only Yosemite feature named after this man whose name is so connected to the park.

Q. How did the Merced River get its name?
A. On September 29, 1806, as a Spanish expedition under the leadership of Gabriel Moraga crossed the river in the San Joaquin Valley, they named it El Rio de Nuestra Señora de Merced (The River of Our Lady of Mercy). This was five days after the annual fiesta that honors her. Later the name was shortened to Merced. It's said that the Indian name for the river was Wa-kal'-la. Tuolumne is thought to be an Indian name meaning "the people of the stone houses."

Q. What two park peaks are named after women?
A. Mt. Florence was named after Florence Hutchings, the first non-Indian child born in Yosemite. Mt. Amelia Earhart was named in 1968 after the famous aviator.

Q. How did Lost Bear Meadow get named?
A. In 1957, a large search party looked for a young girl who had gotten lost near Bridalveil Meadow. When she was found unharmed after three days, she said, "I am not lost, but the bear is lost. He went away and got lost."

*"[Yosemite] is by far the grandest of all the special temples of Nature I was ever permitted to enter."—John Muir*

## *Puzzlers*

### YOSEMITE ELEVATION MATCH

Match the location with correct elevation

| | |
|---|---|
| 1. Yosemite Valley | 13,114 ft. |
| 2. Glacier Point | 8,842 ft. |
| 3. Half Dome | 4,000 ft. |
| 4. Mt. Lyell | 8,600 ft. |
| 5 Tuolumne Meadows | 2,100 ft. |
| 6. Tioga Pass | 10,845 ft. |
| 7. Wawona | 9,941 ft. |
| 8. Mariposa Grove | 7,214 ft. |
| 9. Mt. Hoffman | 4,000 ft. |
| 10. El Portal | 5,600 ft. |

*Mt. Hoffman's crest on a 19th-century stereoscope card.*

### JOKE

Q. Why did the hiker ignore the danger sign at the cliff?
A. He thought it was a bluff.

---

*The Sierra Nevada region is home to more than 3,500 native plant species, about half of those found in California.*

## Quote Quest #1

*Find the underlined words in eight different directions from this quote by John Muir describing how it was glaciers, not an earthquake or some other catastrophic event that created Yosemite Valley:* "**Nature** **chose** for a **tool**, not the **earthquake** or **lightning** to **rend** and **split** **asunder**, not the **stormy** **torrent** or **eroding** **rain**, but the **tender** **snow-flowers** noiselessly through unnumbered **centuries**." *When all the clues have been circled, the remaining letters will spell what mountaineer and minister Thomas Starr King,said about Yosemite.*

```
G L E G N I D O R E R E
S I F A A S T O O L Y T
E G L I R S N G R A M E
I H O N I T T O E A R R
R T W N T D H Y W O O U
U N E R S N E Q E M T T
T I R I E S E T U R S A
N N S E O D I R E A N N
E G S H I T N N R I K S
C P C R O P D U A O H E
E T T I L P S R S W T Q
T E N D E R L K L A H K
```

Hidden message: "_ _ _ _ _  _ _  _ _ _ _ _ _  _ _ _

_ _ _ _ _ _ _ _  _ _  _ _ _  _ _ _ _ _ _ _"

---

*In 1867 Muir walked from Indianapolis to Florida, a trip of 1,000 miles.*

# GEOLOGY

Q. Most of Yosemite rock is granite.
1) True    2) False
A. False. Most of the rock that is taken for granite is actually granodiorite or quartz monzonite. Rocks that are related to granite are known as granitic rocks. True granite, found on the face of El Capitan and near Soda Springs in Tuolumne Meadows, is the hardest of the granitic group.

Q. How is true granite different from granitic rocks?
A. Granite contains almost equal amounts of quartz, potassium feldspar and plagioclase feldspar. Granodiorite and quartz monzonite both contain a larger proportion of plagioclase feldspar and are weaker rocks. The weakest granitic rocks are diorites, which are mostly composed of plagioclase feldspar with a small percentage of quartz and potassium feldspar. Diorite erodes easily, as can be seen in the area east of El Capitan, aptly named "the Rockslides."

Q. What percentage of bedrock in Yosemite is granitic?
1) 50%   2) 75%   3) over 90%

A. 3) More than ninety percent of Yosemite bedrock is in the granite group.

Q. What are the main components of granite?
1) feldspar 2) quartz 3) gold 4) mica
A. 1), 2), and 4). Gold occurs in quartz veins where granitic rock contacts metamorphic rock.

Q. How is granite different from volcanic rocks?
A. Both granitic rock and volcanic rock—such as obsidian, andesite, pumice, and rhyolite—are classified igneous. Igneous rock originates as molten rock from deep within the Earth. Volcanic rocks form above the surface or just below the surface of the Earth, while granitic rocks cool thousands of feet below. The granitic rock of the Sierra Nevada is thought to have crystallized when it was 25,000 feet or more beneath the surface.

Q. How can different granitic rocks be identified by looking at them?
A. It is possible to note relative differences such as size of crystals or higher proportions of light or dark crystals. For example, in Tuolumne Meadows, Johnson Peak granite is fine-grained compared to the more abundant Cathedral Peak granodiorite, which has a higher proportion of dark minerals and large feldspar crystals, some an inch long.

Q. How do these different granitic rocks form?
A. As magma surges up from deep within the Earth, each mass of molten rock or pluton contains a distinct chemical composition and cools at a different rate. Plutons are also of different sizes.

Q. Where are the largest plutons located in the park?
A. Cathedral Peak granodiorite, which is easily identified by its large feldspar crystals, is found from Babcock Lake in the south all the way north to Tower Peak at the northern tip of the park, and around to Mt. Conness on the northeastern boundary. Half Dome granodiorite, with its a distinct salt and pepper appearance, is found from south of Glacier Point, north to Tilden Lake and east to Volgesang Peak. Both of these granodiorites are the "granites" that most people will

*Yosemite's boundaries exclude areas where there were active gold mines in the 19th century.*

think they see in the park.

**Q.** Where are the oldest rocks in Yosemite?
**A.** For years geologists believed the oldest rocks in the Yosemite region were in the lower Merced River canyon on the western side of the park. They even placed a roadside sign near the outcrop of banded cherts stating that these were the most ancient rocks in the park region. In the 1980s,

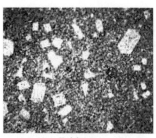

*Feldspar*

geologists from the U.S. Geological Survey collected limestone rock adjacent to these "ancient chert beds." Inside it were fossils of marine worms that lived about 180 million years ago, showing that the chert was actually younger than the metamorphic bedrock on the eastern edge of the park near Tioga Pass. That rock is more than 250 million years old.

**Q.** How does the age of Yosemite rock compare to that of other parks?
**A.** The oldest rock in Yosemite is less than half as old as the rock in Acadia National Park in Maine and Yellowstone National Park, Wyoming.

**Q.** Where are the youngest rocks in the park?
**A.** Little Devil's Postpile, a series of hexagonal columns—an outcrop of the volcanic rock basalt—along the river below Tuolumne Meadows, is 9 million years old. Tiny fragments of obsidian and pumice (a porous rock that can float), that were spewed from the Mono Craters (east of the park boundary) 600 years ago, can be found along the peaks and ridges on to the eastern edge of the park.

---

*Obsidian is found all over Yosemite National Park—*
*but none of it was formed here!*

## Half Dome's Missing Half

Josiah Whitney, appointed California State Geologist in 1860, believed that the Yosemite Valley had been formed by a sudden subsidence and that Half Dome was evidence of this. The missing half simply collapsed into the chasm, he thought. Whitney's assistants had noted signs of glacial action in Yosemite Valley, as well as in the high country, but Whitney disregarded glaciers as a significant factor in shaping the Yosemite Valley. John Muir rejected Whitney's theory, saying that "the bottom never fell out of anything God made." Muir was convinced that a glacier was responsible for the valley's steep walls and waterfalls, and had removed the missing part of Half Dome. Whitney dismissed Muir as a "mere sheepherder" and an "ignoramus." Eventually, other geologists such as Professor Joseph LeConte, of the University of California, agreed with Muir. Today's geologists say Yosemite Valley was changed (from a steep-walled river canyon into its present form with steep walls and waterfalls) by a series of massive glaciers that moved through over a period of thousands of years. Half Dome is composed of rock jointed like slices of a bread loaf. As its lower jointed layers were plucked away by glaciers, the upper layers collapsed. Viewed from the valley, Half Dome does appear to be half of a dome. However, when viewed from Glacier Point it can be seen that it is actually three-quarters of a dome.

Q. Glacial valleys are typically U-shaped in cross section. Why isn't Yosemite Valley U-shaped?

A. More than 10,000 years ago, after the last glacier flowed into Yosemite Valley, it melted and deposited a large terminal moraine (a massive pile of rocks, dirt, and ice) at the east end of the valley. As the glacier melted, the terminal moraine dammed the river and flooded the valley, creating a deep lake. Over the following years the lake slowly filled up with silt until it became a flat valley floor. Perhaps Whitney was fooled by the atypical shape of the valley, but Muir was not.

---

*Paiute Indians brought obsidian to the west side of the Sierra crest, using it to fashion arrow- and spearheads, scrapers, and knives.*

Q. What evidence of glaciers did Muir find to support his ideas?
A. He came across a large chunk of Cathedral Peak granodiorite near Bridalveil Fall. The closest source of this rock is over 15 miles upriver from the Valley. He believed a piece of rock as big as this one could only be carried by a glacier. He also noted the moraines in the west end of the valley and the moraine between Tenaya Creek and the Merced River at the base of Half Dome.

Q. What did Muir discover in 1871 that further supported his glacial theory?
A. In October of 1871 he came upon a glacier in the Clark Range in the upper Merced River drainage. The article Muir wrote for the *New York Tribune* about this discovery created great excitement. Europeans had boasted about having glaciers—now America had one! This was the beginning of Muir's writing career as well as of his fame.

Q. Does the glacier discovered by Muir in the Clark Range still exist?
A. No. The glacier, named Black Mountain Glacier, had melted by 1977.

Q. At the height of the Ice Age, what was the largest glacier in the Sierra Nevada?
A. The Tuolumne Glacier was sixty miles long, stretching from just below the highest peaks to the 2,000-foot level in the Sierra foothills. Its maximum depth was over 4,500 feet.

Q. What do Disneyland, Switzerland, and Yosemite have in common?
A. Each has a Matterhorn peak.
   Yosemite's Matterhorn Peak is on the northeast corner of the park. Like its Swiss namesake, it is a glacial horn. This type of peak is formed when glaciers on several sides of a mountain quarry away rock, leaving a pointed peak behind. During the maximum height of the Tuolumne Glaciation, the peaks of Cathedral, Unicorn, and Matterhorn would have appeared as pointed rocks rising out of a massive ice field.

---

*John Muir Day in California is April 21 (Muir's birthday), and he was the first person honored in this way by the state legislature.*

**Q.** Lembert, Pothole, and other domes are examples of another glacially sculpted feature that is named after sheep and a wig. What is that?

**A.** Lembert Dome is a classic example of a *roche mountonée*, which means rock sheep. An 18th century Swiss mountain climber thought these domes not only looked like sheep, but also like a stylish men's wig that was pomaded with tallow. Roche mountonées have a gentle slope on the up valley side and are steep faced on the down valley side. They are formed when glaciers flow up over the dome and quarry away rock as they speed over the downhill side.

**Q.** Sawtooth Ridge in the Northeast part of Yosemite is a textbook example of which feature?

1) col   2) arête   3) horn

*Arete*

**A.** 2) An arête. When glaciers quarry rock away on both sides of a ridge, they can leave behind a knife-edge ridge, dubbed by geologists with the French term, arête. A gap between teeth on an arête is called a col. Another amazing arête is the Matthes Crest in the Cathedral Range, not far from Sunrise High Sierra Camp. This arête has vertical walls 2,000' high and is narrower than a sidewalk along some parts of its ridgeline.

**Q.** What is an erratic and where are good places to find them?

**A.** When a boulder is carried in a glacier far from its source bedrock and deposited on a different type of bedrock it is known as an erratic. Look for rounded boulders at Olmstead Point or on Pothole Dome in Tuolumne Meadows, which are composed of rock that looks different from the rock they rest on.

**Q.** Before the Ice Age there were few lakes in the Sierra Nevada. How do glaciers create lakes?

**A.** Glaciers form high on mountainsides where snow accumulates year after year until it compacts into ice. As gravity pulls this ice downward, it plucks away rock from behind and underneath

---

*Two first-class U.S. stamps have honored Muir: a 5¢ version including redwoods issued in 1964, and a 32¢ stamp portraying Muir in the Yosemite Valley, released in 1998.*

it. Over time, a glacial cirque is cut from the mountaintop—recognizable by its bowl-shaped depression with a steep wall at its back. May Lake is a cirque lake. When these bowls fill with water, they are known as cirque lakes or tarns. As glaciers melt and recede, they leave moraines with low-lying areas between them, which fill with water. Dog Lake is an example of this kind of lake. Tenaya Lake was created when glaciers scooped out a basin where jointed rock was easily quarried.

Q. Before the beginning of the ice ages there were few waterfalls in Yosemite. How did the glaciers create waterfalls?
A. There are two types of glacially formed waterfalls:

"Giant staircase falls" are the result of a glacier's creating huge "steps" where large joints or cracks in the rock allow it to remove chunks of rock.

"Hanging valley falls" are created after massive glaciers quarry away the lower sides of a V-shaped valley and leave behind vertical walls. The creeks or rivers then flowing into the valley from above plunge over the steep walls.

*Vernal Fall*

Q. Which falls in Yosemite Valley are examples of giant staircase falls?
1) Yosemite    2) Vernal
3) Nevada
A. 2) and 3) Nevada Fall and Vernal Fall are the two last and steepest steps of a giant staircase that the Merced River follows as it flows down to Yosemite Valley.

Q. Which falls in Yosemite Valley are examples hanging valley falls?
1) Yosemite  2) Bridalveil
3) Ribbon  4) All three
A. 4) All three of the above falls, plus Sentinel Falls and Illilouette Fall, flow from gentle creek valleys and then plunge off a cliff

---

*Today, only two glaciers exist within the park's boundary:*
*Lyell and MacClure.*

when they reach the edge of Yosemite Valley. Thus they are all hanging valley falls.

Q. Which geologist completed the first comprehensive photographic surveys of the Sierra Nevada glaciers?
1) Karl Grove Gilbert
2) Joseph LeConte
3) Israel Russell
A. 1) Gilbert, who was a United States Geological Survey geologist for over three decades and was one of the most prominent geologists of his time.

*K.G. Gilbert was his byline.*

Q. What did geologist Francois Matthes contribute to the knowledge of the geologic history of Yosemite?
A. Not only did Matthes map Grand Canyon and Yosemite national parks, among others, but he also confirmed that glaciers

were a major force in shaping Yosemite Valley, and found evidence that there were at least three major glacial periods in the Sierra. His report, *The Geologic History of Yosemite Valley*, was published in 1930.

*Francois Matthes and wife Edith*

---

*Around 1900, Lyell Glacier was four times the size that it was a century later!*

# WATERFALLS

**Q.** Yosemite Falls is the highest falls in
1) North America   2) the world   3) the Northern Hemisphere
4) North *and* South America
**A.** 1) Not only is Yosemite Falls (at 2,450' total for upper and lower falls) the highest in the United States, but it is also higher than any other falls in North America.

**Q.** Angel Falls in Venezuela is the world's highest waterfall. Where does Yosemite Falls rank among the top ten highest waterfalls in the world?
**A.** Worldwide it ranks number four, and Sentinel Falls (Yosemite's second highest) ranks eighth. These two are the only North American falls included in the list of the planet's top ten waterfalls. Norway has four of the ten and Venezuela has two. Tugela Falls in South Africa stands at second place, and Sutherland Falls in New Zealand is ninth tallest.

**Q.** Yosemite has more than 10 waterfalls with a height of over 1,000 feet.
1) True   2) False
**A.** 1) True. Eight of these falls are in Yosemite Valley, one of the ten is Chilnualna Falls in Wawona and the other is Wapama Falls in Hetch Hetchy Valley.

**Q.** Why are some waterfalls named "fall" but others are called "falls"?
**A.** Plural indicates that the water meets one or more obstacles as it falls. Each section of flowing water is called a "drop."

*Yosemite Falls from Glacier Point*

**Q.** The two falls in Yosemite National Park with the largest volume of water are:
1) Yosemite and Bridalveil
2) Sentinel and Wapama
3) Vernal and Nevada
**A.** 3) Vernal and Nevada Fall both contain the waters of the Merced River, which is a larger volume than any of the creeks which feed other major falls.

*Yosemite Falls
in the dry season.*

**Q.** Yosemite Falls originates from:
1) a lake at the rim of the valley   2) the Yosemite River
3) a lakes basin on the north side of Mt. Hoffman
**A.** 3) On the north side of Mt. Hoffman are glacially carved lakes and massive snowfields that feed Yosemite Creek. On the south side of the peak is May Lake, which is the headwaters for Snow Creek and Snow Creek Falls.

---

*Yosemite National Park has more than 25 waterfalls
with heights of over 100 feet.*

Q. Yosemite Falls is usually at its fullest during:
1) winter   2) spring   3) summer   4) fall
A. 2) The peak of snow melt is during spring, and thus the falls are fullest at this time. Some falls, such as Yosemite Falls, are often dry by the end of August and remain that way until rains resume in late autumn.

Q. Which falls can you reach by a trail?
1) Yosemite   2) Ribbon   3) Vernal   4) Nevada
A. 1), 3), and 4). Of the above, only Ribbon Fall is *not* accessible by trail.

Q. What are the highest falls in Hetch Hetchy?
A. Wapama Falls is 1,100 feet high. Tueeulala Falls drops 880 feet and Rancheria is only 30 feet high, but still is very impressive because of its high volume.

Q. Frazil ice is:
1) slush-like collection of needle-shaped ice crystals
2) flavored crushed ice sold in the park
3) cracked river ice
A. 1) In late winter and early spring, when nighttime temperatures are below freezing, the super-cooling of water plunging over Yosemite's waterfalls may lead to formation of a slush-like accumulation of needle shaped crystals called frazil ice. This oily-looking ice often clogs the main creek channel of creeks below Yosemite's waterfalls, forcing water and ice to follow or create a new channel.

---

*Bridalveil Fall was known by the Ahwahneechee as Pohono, and Yosemite Falls was called Chó-lok. The legends for both falls refer to evil or dangerous winds.*

## *Puzzlers*
### QUOTE QUEST #2

*Find the underlined words in eight different directions from this Helen Sharsmith quote, from an article in the* Yosemite Nature Notes *in 1937:* "In May, June, or even July when the **waters** of **Yosemite** **Creek** **shoot** thunderingly over the **brink** of the **valley** rim on the **night** when the **moon** is **full**, then is the time to climb the **zigzags** of the Yosemite Falls trail in search of the **lunar** **rainbow**." *When all the clues have been circled, the remaining letters will spell out what William Brewer of the Whitney Survey wrote in a letter about Bridalveil Falls.*

```
Z  T  H  T  H  G  I  N  E  E
I  S  C  R  E  E  K  T  S  T
G  R  R  E  A  M  I  B  E  W
Z  E  N  T  I  M  V  R  R  O
A  T  E  L  E  A  Y  I  D  B
G  A  I  S  L  S  R  N  S  N
S  W  O  L  S  A  O  K  L  I
L  Y  E  N  N  H  V  E  L  A
S  Y  I  U  O  N  O  T  U  R
O  S  L  P  R  O  A  O  F  Y
C  H  G  K  T  G  M  V  T  K
```

*Hidden message:* "\_ \_ \_  \_ \_ \_ \_ \_ \_  \_ \_ \_ \_ \_ \_ \_ \_

\_ \_ \_ \_ \_ \_ \_ \_ \_  \_ \_ \_ \_  \_ \_ \_ \_ \_"

---

*Spring runoff sometimes sends so much water over Wapama Falls, in Hetch Hetchy Valley, that water overflows the footbridges at the base of the waterfall.*

## Falls Match

Match the heights of these waterfalls with the heights in the second column.

|  |  | *Height* |
|---|---|---|
| 1. | Yosemite Falls | 620 feet |
| 2. | Sentinel Falls | 1,250 feet |
| 3. | Illilouette Fall | 1,300 feet |
| 4. | Vernal Fall | 2,000 feet |
| 5. | Nevada Fall | 370 feet |
| 6. | Ribbon Fall | 594 feet |
| 7. | Royal Arch Cascade | 2,425 feet |
| 8. | Staircase Falls | 317 feet |
| 9. | Bridalveil Fall | 1,000 feet |
| 10. | Horsetail Fall | 1,612 feet |

## Joke

Q. How did Bridalveil Fall get its name?
A. When you get too close you get a wetting.

*Horsetail Fall*

*Horsetail Fall, dropping from El Capitan, is situated so that it "flames" orange (by reflecting the setting sun) during the last half of February.*

# FLOODS, ROCKSLIDES &
# EARTHQUAKES

*Merced River flood, 2005*

## Floods

**Q.** How many major floods have occurred in the Yosemite Valley since the beginning of the 1860s?

1) two   2) four   3) eight

**A.** 3) Eight major floods occurred in the years 1862, 1867, 1871, 1937, 1950, 1955, 1964, and 1997. Most of these floods were the result of warm, wet winter rainstorms saturating and washing away snow from the higher elevations. Such storms usually came from the South Pacific, where they picked up large amounts of moisture. Hence they were dubbed "pineapple express" storms.

**Q.** How long did it take to repair Highway 140 when it was closed after the 1937 flood?

1) one week   2) one month   3) two years

**A.** 3) It took two years to fix road damage and get normal traffic flowing. Sixty years later, after the flood of January 1997, Yosemite

Valley was closed to tourists for three months. Road repairs took two and a half years to finish.

**Q.** During that same 1997 flood, the peak flow at Pohono Bridge on the west end of the valley was:
1) 9,000 cfs    2) 12,300 cfs    3) 25,000 cfs
**A.** 3) That peak flow was 25,000 cubic feet per second, making it two-and-a-half times as great as the Happy Isles flow. That difference was because of the addition of floodwaters from Tenaya, Yosemite, Sentinel, Bridalveil, Ribbon and other smaller creeks, which all enter the Merced in Yosemite Valley below Happy Isles.

**Q.** In what park location have scientists found evidence of major droughts that occurred during the past thousand years?
**A.** In Tenaya Lake there are two sets of submerged dead trees that once grew around the shore when it reached a much lower level during two major droughts, one ending around AD 1100 and the other AD 1350. The trees that are rooted the deepest, almost 70 feet below the present lake surface, grew during the first drought. Using carbon dating, scientists determined that the trees were at least 200 years old when they died, indicating that the first drought lasted for over 200 years. Data from the second set of trees show that the second drought lasted for at least 50 years.

**Q.** When did the largest avalanches of the 20th century occur in the park?
**A.** In February of 1986 numerous avalanches swept away white-bark pines that were at least 1,000 years old. This was a pineapple express storm, but colder than the ones that cause major floods. Over 6 feet of heavy wet snow piled up on top of a base of 5 feet before it slid. This massive amount of snow created avalanches that extended beyond the usual boundaries of avalanche zones.

## Earthquakes

**Q.** What major earthquake did John Muir experience in Yosemite?
**A.** The Lone Pine Earthquake, which occurred on March 26, 1872. He watched Eagle Rock, on the south rim of the valley, fall along with many other large boulders. After witnessing this event Muir

---

*During its 1997 flood, the Merced River's peak flow at Happy Isles was 10,000 cubic feet per second—28 times its normal volume.*

was convinced that the talus slopes—boulder piles at the bases of cliffs—had all been created by earthquakes. Though earthquakes will certainly help create talus piles, rockslides do occur without any earth tremors. Solid rock faces slowly fracture over time and fall apart.

Q. Did the Lone Pine Earthquake damage structures?
A. The epicenter of this quake was near the small town of Lone Pine, California, in the Owens Valley on the eastern side of the Sierra. Most of the houses in town were destroyed and twenty-seven people died. Geologists estimate that the quake was similar in magnitude to the San Francisco earthquake of 1906.

Q. Was there damage to buildings in Yosemite Valley?
A. Since the epicenter was so far away, buildings shook, but were not destroyed. For the next couple of months there were aftershocks that Muir observed by watching the movement of water in a bucket on his table.

## Rockslides

*North Tower across a talus slope, in a drawing from one of John Muir's books*

Q. Where did the biggest rockslide in Yosemite National Park occur?
A. Slide Canyon, north of the Tuolumne River, is the site of this massive rockslide. The rock dropped over 1,500 from the east side of the canyon and traveled over 100 feet up the other side. It is estimated that the velocity of this slide was thousands of miles per hour. The area covered by this slide is greater than the area covered by the Dubai International Airport, the largest airport in the world.

Q. When did this slide occur?
1) 12th century     2) 14th century
3) 18th century
A. 3) Geologists have determined

---

*Between 1857 and 2003, 12 people have been killed as the result of rockslides in the Yosemite Valley, and another 62 injured.*

by dendro-chronology testing of two samples of wood—recovered from logs pinned beneath boulders within the deposit—that the slide occurred between AD 1739 and 1740.

Q. What two park roads are permanently closed due to rockslides?
1) Old Big Oak Flat   2) Coulterville   3) Old Glacier Point
A. 1) & 2). A large rockslide in the spring of 1945 on the north side of Yosemite Valley resulted in permanent closure of the Old Big Oak Flat Road.

In April 1982 the 35 million cubic-foot Cookie Cliff Slide demolished the section of the Coulterville Road on the slope above its junction with highway 140. The highway was closed for several months and the park sewer line was severed. Students from Yosemite Valley had to disembark on the uphill side, cross the partially cleared debris, and board another bus to reach their high school in Mariposa.

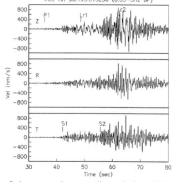

Q. How much rock came down in Happy Isles rockslide on July 10, 1996?
A. As much as 1 million cubic feet of rock plunged 1,500 feet from the cliffs to the west. This was the equivalent of 80,000 full-sized automobiles racing downhill at nearly three times the freeway speed limit.

*Seismograph recording of the 1996 Happy Isles rockslide.*

Q. How many trees toppled from the air blast created by this slide?
1) 300   2) 1,000   3) 3,000
A. 2) Many of the 1,000 trees snapped, but others toppled because of roots weakened by root disease. The root disease was the result of increased forest density caused by fire suppression. With more trees in the area, there was less water and sunlight, and the trees were more susceptible to natural pathogens.

Q. How many people were killed when the Happy Isles snack bar was crushed by these toppled trees?
1) none   2) one   3) eight

*The 1996 Happy Isles rockslide set off seismographs as far away as 118 miles.*

**A.** 2) The young man who was serving customers at the snack stand that day decided to close up early shortly before the rockslide occurred. Thus there weren't any customers there at the time the slide occurred and only one person standing nearby was killed.

**Q.** What lodging complex in Yosemite Valley was built on the talus from prehistoric rockslides?
1) Yosemite Lodge    2) the Ahwahnee    3) Curry Village
**A.** 3) Curry Village was built in the shade of the cliffs below Glacier Point. This was a cooler place to stay during hot summer days, but as the number of tent cabins increased they were built on talus piles, which are rock terraces, created by old rockfalls. These talus slopes contain rocks of various dimensions, from the size of footballs to that of cabins. From 1998 to 2008 there were numerous rock falls in upper part of Curry Village. On November 16, 1998, a rock fall, with a volume equivalent to 42 dump-truck loads of rock, fell from below Glacier Point and hit the top of the talus. Another smaller slide occurred in May 25, 1999, and on June 13, 1999, yet another rock fall occurred to the eastern edge of Curry

*Rockslide of October 2008 aims at Curry Village (top right).*

Village, killing one rock climber and injuring two others. Large football-sized rocks reached tent cabins, breaking beams and slicing through canvas. Three people were injured by the falling rock, but there were no fatalities. In response to this event, 77 employee tent cabins and 132 guest cabins within the area hit by rock were vacated. There were periodic smaller rock falls in this area through July 21, 1999. Almost ten years later, on October 7 and 8, 2008, two new rock falls with a volume equivalent to 570 dump trucks of rock crashed into cabins and other structures. In November the park service decided to close about one third of the cabins at the village.

*Yosemite rocksides have destroyed property, injured visitors, and even killed a climber.*

Q. How many rockfalls occurred in the park in 2009?
1) 25  2) 41  3) 52
A. 3) The largest of the 52 rock falls during this year was the Ahwiyah Point rock fall on March 28, which came from near the summit of Ahwiyah Point on the northeast side of Half Dome. It was almost twice the volume of the Happy Isles slide. This slide closed the southern section of the Mirror Lake loop trail. On August 26 a series of five rock falls came from midway up the Rhombus Wall, near the Royal Arches. Large boulders reached the edge of the existing talus slope, and several vehicles in the Ahwahnee Hotel parking lot were damaged by smaller rock fragments. The hotel was evacuated for 48 hours. Twenty-nine parking spaces in the Ahwahnee parking lot were permanently closed as a result of these rock falls.

## Puzzlers

### GEOGRAPHY & GEOLOGY CROSSWORD
All answers are found in the previous 4 chapters.

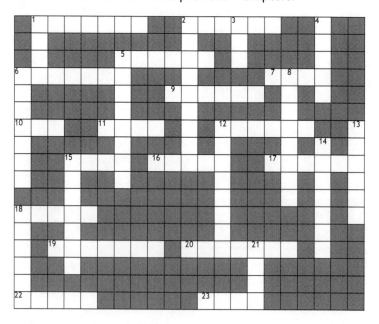

*In the past century and a half, Yosemite has experienced more than 600 rockfalls.*

**Across**
1. Rocks and soil carried along the front and side of a glacier
2. Porous volcanic rock that can float
5. Waterfalls in Yosemite Valley are fullest during this season
6. Igneous rock with equal parts of quartz, potassium feldspar, and plagioclase feldspar
7. Valuable metal that can be found in quartz veins at the contact of granitic and metamorphic bedrocks
9. Volcanic rock that can be found in hexagonal columns
10. Gap in a sawtooth ridge
11. Common shiny mineral found in granite
12. A slush-like collection of needle-shaped ice crystals that forms in super-cooled water
15. Large rounded rock feature
16. Highest peak in Yosemite National Park
17. Lake in Yosemite Valley created by a rockslide damming Tenaya Creek
18. Rock of various sizes found in piles at the base of cliffs
19. Geologist who believed that Yosemite Valley was created by a single cataclysmic down-dropping of the valley floor
20. Chunk of bedrock carried and then deposited by a glacier miles from its point of origin
22. Knife edge ridge created by glaciers
23. Pointed peak created by glaciers quarrying away rock below its summit

**Down**
1. He was the first white to locate a glacier in Yosemite
2. Warm wet storm from the South Pacific that can result in floods or avalanches
3. Geologic Age when waterfalls and lakes were created in Yosemite
4. Canyon with the park's most massive rockfall
5. Second highest waterfall in the park
6. River of ice that moves over land
8. Volcanic rock found in small pieces in the park that was carried from east of the park by the first inhabitants of the Sierra
12. Major component of granitic rock
13. River that flows over Vernal and Nevada Fall
14. Volcanic features to the east of Tioga Pass
15. Long dry spell
21. Lake in glacially carved basin

---

*Yosemite's largest rockslide in historical times occurred in March 1987, when 1.5 million tons of debris fell at the base of Three Brothers, and blocked Northside Drive.*

# PLANTS & TREES

## Plants

Q. How many plant species are in the Yosemite National Park?
1) 853   2) 1002   3) 1450
A. 3) There are 1,450 species of trees, shrubs, wildflowers, and ferns and their allies. The greater park area, which includes the eastern side of the crest down to Mono Lake and west into the lower Merced and Tuolumne River canyons, plus the park, is home to well over 2,000 species.

Q. How many of this total number of species are ferns, club mosses, and horsetails?
1) fifteen   2) thirty-one   3)  forty-five
A. 3) Yosemite has 45 species in this group of early-evolved plants. In comparison, Glacier National Park is home to 62 species of ferns and their allies.

Q. Yosemite has more plant species than which of the following national parks?
1) Yellowstone   2) Grand Canyon   3) Acadia

A. 1) & 3) Of these three parks only Grand Canyon National Park has more plant species.

Q. When was the first flora of the park published?
A. Harvey Monroe Hall and Carlotta Case Hall published *A Yosemite Flora* in 1912. It remained the most comprehensive work on the plants of Yosemite for almost ninety years until *An Illustrated Flora of Yosemite National Park* was published in 2001. This new work took over twenty years to complete.

Q. How many major vegetation zones does this book list for the park?
1) two    2) three    3) five
A. 3) The five zones listed are chaparral/ oak-woodland, mixed conifer, montane, sub-alpine, and alpine. The largest in area of the five, the subalpine zone, covers about 469 square miles or more than a third of the park.

*Mountain monkeyflower along a stream*

Q. What percentage of California plant species grow in the park?
1) 8%    2) 24%    3) 34%
A. 2) Yosemite is less than one percent of the land area of California but is home to more than 24% of the state's plant species. California ranks number one among other states in plant diversity, with about 6,000 species. It's estimated that there are more than 20,000 plant species in North America and as many as 400,000 on the planet.

Q. What percent of the park's plant species are native?
A. Over 90%.

Q. How many non-native plant species are in the park?
1) 67    2) 130    3) 145
A. 2) The 130 non-native plant species in Yosemite are only 9% of the total park flora. Non-native plants comprise about 30% of the plant species in California.

---

*Bracken fern, which grows at Yosemite's mid-elevations, is one of the first plants to sprout after a wildfire. They grow on every continent except Antarctica.*

Q. How many of the total number of native plants species are rare or sensitive?
1) 88    2) 109    3) 160
A. 2) Of the 1320 native species in Yosemite, 109 or 8% are considered rare or sensitive and in need of monitoring.

Q. Which plant has the most species in the park?
A. Sedges, with over 75 species. These grass-like plants are a major component of many park meadows. Tompkin's Sedge is listed as a rare plant species by the State of California. This sedge has become more abundant after fires occurred in its habitat.

Q. How many plant species are named after Yosemite?
A. Eight. They are the Yosemite tarweed, Yosemite onion, Yosemite bitterroot, Yosemite sedge, Yosemite rock cress, Yosemite woolly sunflower, Yosemite mousetail, and Yosemite bulrush.

Q. How many plant species are named after John Muir?
A. Three. Only one of them, *Ivesia muirii* (Muir's mousetails), grows in Yosemite where he collected it on Mt. Hoffman in 1872. *Erigeron muirii* (Muir's daisy) grows in Alaska and *Carlquista muirii* (Muir's tarplant) grows in the coastal mountains near Monterey and in the Sierra Nevada. Both of these species were first collected by him.

Q. Which botanist, who collected plants in Yosemite, has the most park plants named after him?
A. William Brewer has twelve species of Yosemite plants named after him, including a tiny pink monkeyflower. He collected dozens of plant species new to science while serving as the botanist for the California Geological Survey in the early 1860s. In 1899 he participated in the Harriman Expedition to Alaska along with John Muir and other scientists.

*William Brewer (in chair) and his 1860s field team.*

*Two hundred non-native plant species have found their way into the Sierra Nevada Mountains.*

**Q.** Which botanist, who also served as California Superintendent of Public Education, has ten Yosemite plants named after him?
**A.** Henry Nicholas Bolander.

**Q.** Which wildflower has the greatest number of species in the park?
**A.** There are 35 species of *Mimulus*, commonly called monkey-flower.

**Q.** Are any Yosemite plants poisonous?
**A.** At least 8 species are considered toxic. Poison oak causes a rash, and the other seven (corn lily, death camas, water hemlock, alpine laurel, jimson weed, purple nightshade, red elderberry) have leaves or berries that can cause sickness or death if ingested. It is best not to eat any plant unless you are sure of its identity.

**Q.** Which Yosemite plant has the largest leaves?
**A.** Indian rhubarb has leaves that can grow up to a meter wide. This stream-loving plant is not related to garden rhubarb, which it resembles, but is in the saxifrage family. Garden rhubarb is in the buckwheat family.

**Q.** Which Yosemite plants have the same name as common spices but are not related to those spice plants?
**A.** California nutmeg and wild ginger. California nutmeg is a conifer, while the spice nutmeg is from a broad-leaved evergreen tree that grows in the tropics. Wild ginger is in the pipevine family, but the spice ginger is from the root of a tropical plant in the ginger family.

**Q.** How many species of orchids grow in the park?
1) three   2) nine   3) fifteen
**A.** Fifteen species of orchids grow in the park, many in moist environments, but several in seasonally arid locations. In comparison, eight species of orchids are found at Crater Lake National Park, while forty-one species grow in Everglades National Park.

**Q.** What new plant species was discovered in the park in 2003?
**A.** The Yosemite bog-orchid (*Platanthera yosemitensis*), which

---

*The oldest known lodgepole pine tree grows in Yosemite, near Tuolomne. According to its rings, it is more than six centuries old.*

*Yosemite bog-orchid*

smells like stinky feet or a horse corral on a hot day, was discovered by a park botanist in a meadow in the southern half of the park.

**Q.** What Yosemite lichen is found on all continents?
**A.** That's map lichen, which is crust-like and chartreuse colored, and grows on rocks. Colonies often have the shape of a continent or island.

**Q.** What is that pink color on alpine snowfields?
**A.** *Chlamydomonas nivalis* is a blue-green algae with red pigment. Differing from most other freshwater algae, it thrives in snow, causing what's called "watermelon snow."

The red pigment absorbs heat from sunlight to help with photosynthesis. When the snow melts the algae is deposited on the ground and then covered with snow. These one-celled algae then swim to the surface of the snowfield in summer to grow. Though it smells like watermelon, it can cause an upset stomach if eaten.

**Q.** What has been the effect of wildfires on rare plants growing in the park?
**A.** In most cases there was an increase in the numbers of these plants. In 1987, after the Stanislaus Complex Fire along the park's northwestern boundary, the very rare Hetch Hetchy monkeyflower was found growing in vast numbers. Its seeds were lying dormant in the soil waiting for the right conditions to germinate. The removal of brush and small trees created the growing conditions it needs. Many of the rare plants that thrive after a fire are "pioneer species."

**Q.** Are there illegal marijuana gardens in the park?
**A.** Since the 1990s, illegal marijuana cultivation on public lands, including parks, has become more common. In 2007 national park and forest service rangers, in collaboration with state and county law enforcement officers, raided four illegal gardens

---

*"Pioneer species" are plants that re-colonize disturbed lands—not just after fires, but also after avalanches, rockslides, and even damage by animals.*

along the boundary of the park and national forest. Over 14,000 plants were seized, valued at $43 million. In 2009 authorities eradicated another 4,700 plants with estimated value of $19 million. Currently, illegal cultivation of marijuana is the most serious destructive activity in the park. Clearing vegetation, ditching and damming streams, accumulating trash and human waste, and use of fertilizer all degrade park resources.

## Trees and Shrubs

Q. How many species of trees grow in Yosemite?
1) twenty-one   2) twenty-nine   3) forty-nine
A. At 49 tree species, Yosemite has half the number of tree species found in Great Smoky Mountain National Park and six times the number found in Denali National Park.

Q. How many of these species are conifers?
1) three   2) eleven   3) seventeen
A. 3) With 17 conifer species, Yosemite has double the number found in Yellowstone.

Q. Which tree looks like a sequoia and, though it is called a cedar, is not a true cedar?
A. The incense cedar (*Calocedrus decurrans*), a relative of cedars, with leaves and wood with an incense-like scent. Many people confuse this tree with giant sequoias because they have similar bark. Incense cedar is unique to the western United States. One of the other two species of Calocedrus is native to Taiwan and the other to Southeast Asia.

*Incense cedar*

Q. What Yosemite conifer is found all across the northern hemisphere?
A. Dwarf juniper (*Juniperus communis*), a shrub form that grows only at tree line in Yosemite.

---

*Pine trees, with eight species present in the park, are the main conifers in Yosemite's forests.*

Q. Which park tree grows across northern Asia, Europe, as well as across North America?
A. Mountain alder (*Alnus incana*) has two to three subspecies, and grows in moist areas.

Q. Which tree is found only in the Merced Gorge at the park's lowest elevation?
A. Oregon ash is a common tree along the Merced River west of the park, but only a few specimens grow within the park boundary.

Q. How many of Yosemite's tree species are willows?
1) three    2) six    3) nine    4) eleven
A. 2) Six of the park's seventeen willow species are trees, the other eleven are shrubs. Two of them, the snow willow and alpine willow, grow in low mats not more than 2" or 3" tall. Yosemite's two cottonwood species, black and Fremont's, and trembling aspen are in the same family as willows.

Q. Like conifers and alders, willows and poplars thrive in northern areas. Which Yosemite tree is tropical in origin?
A. The California bay laurel tree is in the same plant family as avocados. The majority of species in the laurel family are in southern Asia and Brazil. Their leaves can be used for seasoning foods, but are more potent than leaves from Mediterranean bay laurels, which are the bay leaves sold in markets.

Q. Which Yosemite trees produce nuts?
1) oaks    2)   hazelnut   3) sugar pine
A. 1), 2), and 3) The seeds of all these trees are considered to be nuts. Acorns need to be processed to remove tannins before they are edible.

Q. Which of these of non-native trees were planted in Yosemite by homesteaders?
1) palm  2) elm   3) cypress
A. 2) There is an American elm growing in Cook's Meadow near Yosemite Village.

---

*California has nine other national parks in addition to Yosemite National Park.*

Q. How many species of oak are there in the park?
1) three   2) five   3) seven
A. 3) Yosemite has 7 oak species. Huckleberry oak is a "shrub oak" that grows between elevations of five to eight thousand feet. The three other evergreen oak species, the golden cup oak, interior live oak, and scrub oak, are trees. The remaining three species, California black oak, Brewer's oak, and blue oak, are deciduous. Just outside the park boundary, in El Portal, are groves of valley oaks, the largest oak species in California. Valley oaks can have a trunk diameter of more than 20' and can grow as tall as a twelve-story building. Both canyon live oaks and black oaks can attain similar girth, but don't grow as tall or spread as wide.

*A Paiute woman cleaning acorns during the 1930s*

Q. Which oak was critically important to native people in the park?
A. California black oak acorns were the preferred acorn because of their flavor. Because they have to be completely dry before processing, acorns were stored for a year before being ground and leached to make acorn meal.

Q. Which two park birds depend on acorns for a major portion of their diet?
A. Band-tailed pigeons and acorn woodpeckers eat vast quantities of acorns. The pigeons crack the acorns using their strong, muscular gizzards. Acorn woodpeckers store their prize in "granaries," holes in tree trunks. Steller's and California scrub jays also eat acorns and often bury them for later use. Unrecovered acorn caches are a sources of new oak seedlings.

Q. Yosemite is home to the largest U.S. specimens of what two tree species?
A. Both a champion red fir and a champion white fir grow in the park. The red fir is 172' high and has a circumference of 365". The white fir is 217' with a circumference of 276".

---

*Black bears, mule deer, squirrels, wood rats, and weevils all depend on acorns for part of their diets.*

Q. Why are both of these fir species called widow-makers?
A. They have weak trunks and break during high winds, sometimes killing loggers.

Q. Which tree, photographed by Ansel Adams in 1940, became a Yosemite icon?
A. The image of Jeffrey pine on Sentinel Dome is one of Adam's best known Yosemite photos. A decayed trunk is the only remnant of this tree, which died during the drought of 1976-77.

Q. What Yosemite tree species is found growing at the highest elevations?
A. Whitebark pines are found growing up to tree limit, which is as high as 11,500 feet in the park. The trees growing at the highest elevations look like shrubs because their trunks are lying on the ground and their foliage is pruned by cold

*Whitebark pine*

winter temperatures. At these high elevations their branches may grow only a half inch or less per year.

Q. Which tree species depends on the Clark's nutcracker for its survival?
1) whitebark pine   2) California black oak   3) ponderosa pine
A. 1) Without the nutcracker, the whitebark pines can't regenerate. Unlike other pines, their cones don't open to release the pine seeds. Instead, nutcrackers hammer open the cones, then store up to 150 seeds in pouches under their tongues before flying elsewhere to cache them for winter food. Unrecovered seeds become new trees.

Q. Approximately how many whitebark pine seeds can be cached by an adult Clark's nutcracker in a single season?
1) 1,000   2) 12,000   3) 35,000
A. 3) Scientists have estimated that an adult can cache 35,000 nuts within a couple of months. Harvesting begins in mid-July and continues until the end of summer.

---

*Some whitebark pine trees, like ones growing on Sentinel Dome or in Tuolumne Meadows, grew from seeds carried by Clark's nutcrackers from many miles away.*

Q. Why are campfires illegal above 9,600 feet in the park?
A. The trees not only grow slower at higher elevations, but also their dead wood decays at about the same rate at which they grow. These pines may reach ages of 1,500 or more, thus wood from one of these ancient trees could take almost 1,500 years to decay. In these locations a piece of wood used in a campfire might be thousands of years old and take that long to replace.

Q. Which pine tree is sometimes called a tamarack?
A. Lodgepole pines are sometimes referred to as tamaracks, which are actually larches.

Q. Which tree native to eastern North America and planted by settlers in Yosemite Valley in the 19th century is now rare in the east?
A. The American elm in the meadow between Yosemite Lodge and Yosemite Village is older than many American elms on the east coast, which were devastated by Dutch elm disease in the middle of the 20th century. Another eastern tree planted in the valley and still surviving is a sugar maple growing across from the chapel.

Q. Most conifers that grow in the areas of heavy snowfall are adapted to handle big snow loads. Which conifer is the most flexible?
1) lodgepole pine    2) red fir    3) mountain hemlock
A. 3) Mountain hemlocks are, and can be bent over by snow then spring back into a fairly straight shape after being covered most of the winter. Early-season mountaineers are sometimes bombarded by snow catapulted by hemlock saplings that spring up as the snow melts.

When covered by heavy snow, red fir trees shed snow as their branches lie down from the weight. This is a good reason not to stand under them during or after a snowstorm.

Lodgepole pines are the least flexible, becoming bent and twisted after winters spent under snow.

Q. At the base of some avalanche slopes, which of these trees can be found growing in shrub form?
1) black cottonwood    2) black oak    3) quaking aspen

---

*Pinyon pines growing near Hetch Hetchy Valley mark traditional campsites of Pauite people, who carried the nuts there from east of the Sierra. These were one of their favorite foods.*

**A.** 3) Stunted aspens grow at the bases of avalanche slopes where snow loads deposited in winter provide summer moisture. These trees are twisted by heavy snow loads and their trunks are pruned by avalanches.

**Q.** The heaviest cones are found on which conifer?
1) gray pine     2) sugar pine
3) sequoia
**A.** 1) and 2) Gray pine (*Pinus sabiniana*) cones take two years to mature and can weigh more than two pounds. Their seeds are the largest of any pine species.

*Comparison of sugar pine cones to a giant sequoia cone*

**Q.** Which Yosemite conifer has the longest cone?
**A.** Sugar pine cones can reach a length of two feet.

**Q.** Can you take these cones home as souvenirs?
**A.** No. It's illegal to take anything out of the park. As the saying goes, "take only pictures, leave only footprints."

**Q.** The longest needles are found on this park pine.
1) gray pine    2) ponderosa pine    3) Jeffery pine
**A.** 1) All three of these pines are in the yellow pine group. Gray pines, which grow in the lower elevations of the park, can have needles as long as 12 inches.

**Q.** Which Yosemite conifers are only found growing naturally in California?
1) giant sequoia    2) California nutmeg    3) California bay laurel
**A.** 1) Giant sequoias are the only tree species in the genus *Sequoiadendron*, but are closely related to other "redwoods," the coast redwood and dawn redwood. They are found growing naturally in groves with other sequoias. Merely about 75 groves exist, all of them in the Sierra Nevada, and three in Yosemite. Since their discovery by Euro-Americans they have been planted all over the world. California nutmeg is one of two species in the

---

*Juniper "berries" are actually fleshy cones.*
*They are used to flavor gin.*

genus *torreya*, and the only other native torreya. California nutmeg is endemic to the coast ranges and Sierra Nevada. The other Torreya species, gopherwood, grows in the Florida panhandle and is an endangered species. The California nutmeg native range is the Sierra and California's coastal ranges.

Q. What did a British botanist want to call these big trees?
A. English botanist John Lindley proposed the name Wellingtonia in honor Field Marshal Arthur Wellington, who led British forces to victory against Napoleon at the battle of Waterloo. Instead the big trees and the coast redwood were named after a Cherokee silversmith named Sequoyah who created a writing system for the Cherokee language. Many British still call giant sequoias *wellingtonias*, though the accepted name is *Sequoiadendron gigantea*.

Q. When was the tunnel cut through the Wawona Tunnel Tree in the Mariposa Grove?
1) 1863   2) 1878   3) 1903
A. 2) This popular tourist attraction, created when a tunnel was cut in 1878, thrilled park visitors until it fell during heavy snows in the winter of 1969. Such an act in the park these days would be forbidden.

*Grizzly Giant*

Q. Is the Grizzly Giant in the Mariposa Grove of big trees the largest tree in the world?
A. No, it currently ranks about 25th, with the biggest-tree designation going to the General Sherman tree in Sequoia National Park. The diameter of the Grizzly Giant is 31 feet and its height is 209 feet. The Mariposa Grove's Columbia Tree is 285 feet tall.

---

*In October 1833, Joseph R. Walker and party of trappers and hunters are thought to have been the first whites to see sequoias.*

Q. Are giant sequoias the oldest trees on Earth?
A. At first, many scientists thought that sequoias were the oldest trees on the planet. Though some sequoias are more than 3,000 years old, the Earth's oldest trees are bristlecone pines that grow in the White Mountains of California, which may attain an age of 4,600 years.

Q. Which conifer cone contains the most seeds?
1) lodgepole pine    2) sugar pine    3) sequoia
A. 2) Sequoia, which has an average of 200 seeds per cone.

Q. How many cones can be found on a mature giant sequoia?
1) 1,000    2) 3,700    3) 11,000
A. 3) Each year a mature big tree may produce 2,000 *new* cones, and can hold as many as 11,000 cones at a time.

Q. With an average of 200 seeds in each new cone, how many seeds are produced each year?
A. 400,000. Only one in million seeds finds a suitable place to germinate and grow.

Q. What two animals are most responsible for giant sequoia seed dispersal?
A. The chickaree, a small tree squirrel, and the tiny long-horned beetle (*Phymatodes nitidus*).
    The chickaree eats the cone scales and cuts cones off sequoia trees to store as winter food. The beetle lays her eggs at the junction of the cone scales and the young beetle grubs chew a tunnel into the interior of the cone. This cuts off water to the cones and the scales dry out, causing them to open and drop seeds.

Q. What are the best conditions for sequoia seed germination?
1) sunny and hot    2) cool and dark    3) hot and dark
A. 2) Cool and dark conditions provide the most successful rates of germination. In the first year of growth a sequoia seedling may grow 2 inches, and in the first 100 years may reach heights of 200 feet.

---

*In 1852 some gold prospectors became the first non-Indians to see the Mariposa Grove of giant sequoias.*

After sequoia groves first were set aside in protected preserves, very few new tree seedlings sprouted. Why?

Fires were suppressed within the groves by park rangers who did not know that the seeds needed fire to create a bare mineral seedbed free of harmful fungi. In 1964 Harold Biswell, a professor at U.C. Berkeley, began igniting carefully controlled fires in sequoia groves in an experimental forest next to Sequoia National Park. Biswell and his colleague Harold Weaver discovered that after a fire there were a large number of seedlings and, better yet, the seedlings survived. Instead of natural fires' being harmful to sequoia groves as early park managers believed, they are essential to their continued survival.

**Q.** What prevents a mature sequoia from catching on fire?

**A.** Sequoia bark is highly resistant to fire and acts like a shield when light fires burn through a sequoia grove. On older trees it can be two to three feet thick.

Fire-touched sequoia

**Q.** Do other forests in the park need fires to stay healthy?

**A.** Most of Yosemite's forest communities are adapted to low-intensity surface fires ignited by lightning. The role of fire was understood by some park managers, such as park guardian Galen Clark. He witnessed Indian residents of Yosemite Valley using fire to manage the meadows and oak woodlands. Many of the plants that provided native people with food, medicine, materials for baskets, string, and shelter thrive after fires. Yosemite's first people routinely set fires to favor the growth of these important plants. Soil cores from Yosemite Valley indicate an increase in ash deposits after people began residing here thousands of years ago. As Euro-American people took over the management of park forests and meadows, they began a program of not only forbidding Indian use of fire to manage their forest "crops," but also initiated a policy of putting out lightning-caused fires.

---

*Congress set aside the Mariposa Grove of Big Trees and the Yosemite Valley for protection in 1864, but they were still under the control of California when Yellowstone became the first national park in 1872.*

Aggressive fire suppression began in the 1930s with the available labor of the Civilian Conservation Corps. Finally in the 1950s and '60s the work of fire ecologists, like Biswell and Weaver, led to a shift in park service fire policy.

*Fire in a crowded Yosemite grove of trees.*

Q. When did the National Park Service start its program of using fire to clear fuels in forests and to restore meadows? A. In the early 1970s, park staff began a prescribed-fire program, allowing natural fires to burn when it was determined that fuel and weather conditions would promote a "cool" ground fire. Some of these natural burns were permitted to burn for long periods, as long as conditions stayed stable. Resource rangers also ignited fires for the purpose of restoring plant communities to pre-fire-suppression conditions. Each prescribed burn requires rigorous assessment of fuel moisture and depth, air moisture, and wind speeds before   it can be ignited.

Currently, naturally ignited fires are allowed to burn in 80 percent of the park, which is mostly designated wilderness. In 2007, firefighters conducted prescribed burns on nearly 29,000 acres of national park and let natural fires burn another 43,000 acres.

## Puzzlers

### QUOTE QUEST #3

*Find the underlined words in eight different directions from this quote by Mary Curry Tressidder in her 1932 book* Trees of Yosemite: "From the **first golden shaft** of **sunlight** to the **ruddy glow** of **sunset** one **must** go all **through** the day to **reach** a realization of them." *When all the clues have been circled, the remaining letters will spell what John Muir wrote in a letter about the power of the sequoias.*

---

*Foxtail pines are native to California, but are found in the Klamath Mountains of the Northwest, and in the southern Sierra Nevada, including Yosemite National Park.*

```
C   T   R   T   S   U   M   S   O
M   S   E   U   S   U   C   U   K
T   R   H   S   D   G   E   N   S
H   I   Q   C   L   D   N   L   U
R   F   U   O   A   E   Y   I   N
O   O   W   I   D   E   A   G   S
U   A   N   L   D   B   R   H   E
G   E   O   S   A   V   E   T   T
H   G   S   H   A   F   T   D   M
```

Hidden message: "_ _ _ _   _ _ _ _   _ _ _ _ _ _ _   _ _ _

_ _   _ _ _ _ _."

## TREE ACROSTIC

Y _ _ _ _ _          Three tree species found in the park belong to this group of pines.
O _ _ _ _ _          This ash grows in Yosemite, but is named for another state.
S _ _ _ _ _ _        Tree named after a Cherokee Indian.
E _ _                One specimen of this eastern tree grows in Yosemite Valley.
M _ _ _ _ _ _ _      Name of park big-tree grove.
I _ _ _ _ _ _        A relative of true cedars that is sometime mistaken for sequoias.
T _ _ _ _ _ _ _      An inaccurate name for a lodgepole pine.
E _ _ _ _ _ _ _ _    Four species of Yosemite oaks are in this group.

## JOKES

What flower grows under your nose?
Tulips. (Star tulips grow in Yosemite.)

What tree is easiest to identify by its bark?
Dogwood!

Why is it warmer at Glacier Point than Yosemite Valley?
There are more firs.

---

*Limber pines grow just east of Yosemite's boundary.*

# WILDLIFE

## Mammals

Q How many species of mammals are found in Yosemite National Park? How does this compare to Yellowstone?
1) 63   2) 90   3) 102
A. Though Yellowstone has more large species of mammals, it has 25 fewer mammal species than Yosemite's 90.

Q. How many of these species are not native to the park?
1) two   2) four   3) six   4) eight
A. 2) The park's four non-native mammals are the black rat, house mouse, Virginia opossum, and beaver. Beavers are native to the San Joaquin and Sacramento valleys but were not present in the higher elevations of the western Sierra Nevada rivers. Opossums are native to the southeastern United States. The black rat originated in the Indo-Malaysian Archipelago, and the house mouse most likely originated in northern India.

Q. Which park mammal was first found by scientists in the Yosemite high country?

A. The Mount Lyell shrew is known from three specimens collected in the park near Mount Lyell in 1915, by the Grinnell survey. Later on other specimens were obtained east of Yosemite. This diminutive insect-eater has been found in moist areas near streams, in grass, or under willows.

Q. What order of park mammals has the most species?
1) rodents   2) bats   3) carnivores
A. There are 33 species of rodents in the park, making them largest order of mammals here. This includes 6 species of squirrels, 6 species of chipmunks, and 6 species of mice. The next largest group of mammals in the park are bats, with 17 species living in Yosemite.

Q. Which of these squirrel species hibernates for the longest period?
1) western gray   2) golden-mantled   3) Belding
A. Belding ground squirrels hibernate for up to three-quarters of their lives. Hibernation may last eight months. Females live in separate colonies from males, but are allowed to visit one day out of the year to mate.

Q. Which amphibian overwinters with these squirrels?
A. The Yosemite toad hibernates in the same burrows, but is not molested by the squirrels because it possesses a protective poison gland.

Q. Which of these park squirrel species does not hibernate?
1) Douglas 2) golden-mantled 3) Belding
A. Douglas squirrels, also know as chickarees, stay active all winter. They continue to forage for seeds, but also depend on large caches of conifer seeds, stashed each fall, to survive into spring.

Q. What is the largest rodent species living in Yosemite?
1) beaver   2) marmot   3) porcupine

---

*The Yosemite toad, Sierra Nevada yellow-legged frog, and Pacific fisher (member of the weasel family), are candidates for the endangered or threatened species lists.*

**A.** Beavers are the largest. They can weigh 45 pounds or more and grow up to three and a half feet in length. Porcupines come in second with weights up to 25 pounds and next are yellow-bellied marmots, which weigh up to 11 pounds.

**Q.** If you see a hamster-like animal running in a boulder field, is it someone's pet that got loose?
**A.** No. Pikas, or "rock rabbits," are small hamster-sized mammals that inhabit rock piles at high elevations. Like rabbits, their relatives, they do not hibernate. Unlike rabbits and hares, pikas store piles of dry plants for their winter food. With short ears and skid-resistant foot pads, they are well adapted to living in talus slopes during frigid high-elevation winters.

*Pika*

**Q.** Which mountain mammal is closely related to groundhogs?
1) ground squirrels   2) yellow-bellied marmot
3) mountain beaver
**A.** Marmots live alongside meadows where they graze, but must always have burrows nearby. Burrows are usually built underneath boulders, which the resident marmots rest atop while always keeping a lookout for predators. The creatures don't leave their burrows until May, after the snow has melted enough for them to find food in high meadows.

**Q.** Why is the dusky-footed wood rat also called a pack rat?
1) they wear packs     2) they hoard food and treasures
3) they pack trails in mud
**A.** This species hoards food and treasures in large stick nests in trees, rock piles, and sometimes in the walls or attics of houses.

**Q.** Which thieving mammal was responsible for the disappearance of stuffed-animal exhibits in the Happy Isles Nature Center?
1) wood rat   2) raccoon   3) ringtail cat

---

*When the old Degnan house in Yosemite Valley was demolished, workers discovered acorns, credit cards, jewelry, coins and other items stashed in the walls by pack rats.*

**A.** One spring, rangers opened up the nature center after its winter closure and to their surprise they discovered that the stuffed animal exhibits were missing. There were no signs of a thief forcibly entering the building. However, careful examination revealed the wooden base of one of the stuffed animals sticking out from a hole in the ceiling. A ringtail cat had carried all of the stuffed animals up and into the attic where it ate them, but couldn't fit the last one through the hole! Though dried skin doesn't sound too appetizing to us, it was like beef jerky to the ringtail cat.

**Q.** If you see a chipmunk in Yosemite Valley could it be the same species you might have seen in Tuolumne Meadows?
**A.** No. Each chipmunk species has different habitat requirements. For example, the long-eared chipmunk is found primarily below 6,000 feet in mixed conifer forests and chaparral, while the lodgepole chipmunk lives at higher elevations in open-canopy Jeffrey pine, lodgepole and whitebark pine forests, as well as in mixed conifer forests and higher-elevation chaparral.

**Q.** Which mammal is seldom seen and may die when caught in a cage trap?
**A.** Shrews have such a high metabolism that they can starve in a live trap if they are not recovered promptly. Shrews eat constantly, and can die without eating for five hours or more.

**Q.** How many species of shrews are there in Yosemite?
1) three    2) four    3) five
**A.** All five species of shrews found in the park are primarily mountain residents. Shrews prey on insects, invertebrates and other small animals. They consume 200% to 300% of their body weight each day.

**Q.** What is the most common bat species in the park?
1) big brown    2) pallid    3) Mexican freetail
**A.** Big brown bats are one of the most widely dispersed of bat species, being found from Canada, across the United States and south through the Caribbean Islands to northern South America, including Yosemite. They may have a wing span of over 12 inches.

---

*Yosemite has six species of chipmunks, as compared to Yellowstone's three species and Great Smoky Mountains National Park's one species.*

Q. What is the smallest bat species bat in the park?
1) western pipistrelle   2) western mastiff   3) Mexican freetail
A. 1) That's the tiny western pipistrelle bat, which weighs between 3 to 6 grams (the weight of a large grasshopper), and roosts on rocky cliffs, under loose rocks, or in caves. They often emerge to forage a few hours earlier than other bat species.

Q. What is the largest bat species bat in the park?
1) big brown   2) western mastiff   3) Mexican free tail
A. 2) The western mastiff bat is the largest species found in all the United States. Large individuals may be as long as a bluebird and have a greater wingspan than a jay. Most sightings of this species in California have been in Yosemite, where the bats nest in cliffs.

Q. How many young do most species of bats give birth to at one time?
1) one   2) five   3) eight
A. 1) Most bat species give birth to only one pup at a time. Mama bats may congregate in roosting colonies along with other nursing mothers.

Q. Which park bat species has large roosting colonies?

1) big brown   2) pallid
3) Mexican free tail
A. 3) Mountainous piles of droppings or guano at the bases of cliffs is a telltale sign that a vast number of Mexican free tail bats are residing in cliff cracks. One of the largest colonies in the park was discovered by rock climbers near the base of a climbing route. As many as 400,000 Mexican free tail bats have been found in single roosting locations at

*A Mexican free tail bat in its cliff home*

Carlsbad Caverns National Park, New Mexico.

Q. What species of deer live in Yosemite?
1) white-tailed deer   2) mule deer   3) fallow deer

---

*Six different species of bats may roost in the hollow cavities of Yosemite's giant sequoia trees.*

A. 2) Mule deer, also known as black-tailed deer, are the only deer in the Central Sierra Nevada. They are found at all elevations in the park. In fall they migrate to the lower canyons and in spring they return to the high country.

Q. What is the only park mammal that has killed people?
A. Two park visitors have been killed by deer. A boy was fatally wounded when he was feeding a buck that pierced him with its antlers while it was trying to get more food. Another visitor got too close to a very tame deer to take a photo. This spooked the deer, which struck the person with its hooves. The visitor died from the injury.

Q. Are there wolverines in Yosemite?
A. Park scientists have not been able to confirm if these large members of the weasel family are still in the park. There were confirmed sightings of wolverines by rangers and scientists in 1929 and 1932. Over the years following these sightings, there have been reports by visitors, but none of these were documented with photographs. The most recent photo-documented sighting of a wolverine in California was in Tahoe National Forest in February 2010.

Q. Are coyotes dangerous?
A. In the park some coyotes have learned to beg at the roadsides. It is illegal to feed them and they are dangerous to people who get close enough to them to give them food.

Q. Are tule elk native to Yosemite?
A. No.
   Almost 100 years ago, M. Hall McCallister, the conservation chair at the California Academy of Science, was concerned that tule elk, native to California's Central Valley, would become extinct due to habitat loss from intensive agriculture and the killing by farmers concerned about crop loss. In 1921, he got permission from the Park Service to build a 28-acre fenced paddock in Yosemite Valley for the elk. He started with just a one bull and three cow elk, and then added fourteen more elk the next year. By 1933 there were twenty-eight elk in this herd and it had become a tourist

*Deer, which seem so placid, will defend themselves with razor-sharp hooves if they feel threatened.*

attraction. At the same time, park service rangers realized that the valley was not the best habitat for the elk—or elk grazing the best treatment for the meadows. That fall the elk were transferred to pastures near Bishop, California.

As of 2010 there were more than 2,000 elk living in reserves in the Central Valley and California coast.

Q. What color are Yosemite's black bears?
1) cinnamon    2) blond    3) black    4) any of these
A. 4) Black bears in Yosemite have all three fur colors.

Q. How much does a mature adult black bear weigh?
A. The average weights of adult males is 300-350 pounds, and 200-250 for adult females.

Q. What time of year do bears weigh the most?
1) fall    2) winter    3) spring    4) summer
A. 1) Bears eat enormous quantities of acorns in the fall to gain the fat they need to make it through their winter sleep. They may consume 20,000 calories a day during their period of weight gain. That's the equivalent of eating 70 slices of pizza.

Q. Have bears killed anyone in Yosemite?
A. No people have ever been killed by bears in the park, but people have been injured by bears when they got too close or tried to reclaim a bag or pack from them.

Q. How many cubs are usually in a litter?
A. The average is two but a sow can give birth to more. Litters of six cubs have been reported. Babies are born during the winter in their dens while mom is in a deep sleep. They weigh about eight ounces and are the size of a large candy bar. Sows give birth every two to four years. In low-food years, sows may lose their cubs before birth. Cubs nurse for six months and then learn to forage from their mothers until they are sixteen to seventeen months old.

Q. How many black bears live in the park?
A. It's estimated that there are from 300 to 500.

---

*The biggest black bear ever captured in Yosemite weighed 690 pounds.*

Q. What don't bears eat?
1) grass   2) grubs   3) pine needles   4) wasps
A. 3) Bears eat grass and other vegetation, berries, grubs, acorns and a variety of other foods, but not pine needles.

Q. A black bear can run as fast as
1) 5 mph   2) 10 mph   3) 35 mph
A. 3) Running from a bear is not a good idea unless you can run faster than 35 mph! Bears will chase people who run away, but if you stand tall and yell they tend to back off.

Q. Until the 1960s bears in Yosemite Valley were most likely to be seen in
1) meadows   2) campgrounds
3) park garbage pits
A. 3) As tourist development increased in Yosemite Valley, so did the bear population. Starting around 1910, garbage was collected from the hotels and campgrounds and taken to an enclosure near Camp Curry, where it was used to attract bears onto a platform for viewing. Open garbage dumps, such as one nicknamed "Bear Hill," attracted as many as sixty bears at one time. These became reliable places for tourists to see and photograph bears. By the 1920s, a number of tourists had been injured by these "tame" bears. In response, rangers began luring the bears away from lodgings and campgrounds to garbage dumps, using trails of food scraps. So many park visitors went to these new, more distant, dumps to watch the bears that the park service built a parking area and bleachers.

Q. Are bears still fed in dumps?
A. No!
   The policy of allowing park bears to feed on refuse increased their population. This large number of habituated bears gave rise to more dangerous incidents with visitors. By the 1920s, bears started breaking into vehicles for food. They begged for food

*Ranger naturalists once conducted "bear programs" where they talked about bears while people shined their car headlights on bears wallowing in trash pits.*

along roadsides, where tourists fed them out of their hands. Tourists and even rangers posed next to bears for photographs. By the 1960s, the National Park Service began to re-evaluate management policies and determined that the dumps should be closed. The park service started transporting trash to landfills outside the park. With this abundant source of food gone, the artificially high population of bears started to break into trash cans and cars in earnest.

Q. When did an official National Park Service bear management program start?
A. In 1975 the park service implemented a plan with three main goals:
  1. to get bears back to their natural diet, behavior and population size;
  2. to replace all park dumpsters and trash cans with bear-proof designs;
  3. to educate visitors about bears.

Q. What was the result of twenty years of this management plan?
A. In 1998, there were more than 1,500 bear incidents resulting in $650,000 worth of property damage. Introducing bear-resistant canisters for backpackers, and storage lockers in campgrounds, parking lots, and lodging areas in the 1980s improved things, but the problem still exists. Property damage in 2009 was $80,000.

Q. Who is responsible for continued conflicts with bears?
A. People! Both park residents and visitors need to continually be educated about proper food storage. If people stored food in a consistently proper manner, wildlife managers believe that bears would return to natural behavior and diet. In the past, rangers have killed bears that have become too aggressive. Irresponsible people are the cause of these deaths.

_____

*Speeding cars are one of the greatest dangers to Yosemite's bears and smaller mammals. In 2009, twenty-five bears were killed by cars.*

## *Birds*

Q. How many bird species have been sighted in Yosemite National Park?

A. More than 255 species have been recorded within park boundaries. This is more than one quarter of the bird species in the United States. Every decade, additional species are added to this list.

Q. How many of these species are yearly residents in the park?
1) 114   2) 167   3) 199

A. There are 167 species of birds that can be seen in the park each year. The other 97 species are birds that pass through.

Q. What number of bird species nest in the park?
1) 114   2) 133   3) 199   4) 208

A. Nests of 133 bird species have been located within the park. Some, like those of the gray crowned rosy finch and the water pipit, were the first nests of these species located in the Sierra.

Q. Which species migrate south to reside in the park during winter?

A. Cedar waxwings, varied thrushes and golden-crowned sparrows are seen in Yosemite during winter and into early spring, but migrate north to breed. Populations of American robins that breed in the far north also winter in the park, while robins that nest in the park fly south the Central America. This may be also the case with some other species of songbirds seen in the park year-round.

*Cedar waxwing*

*Steller's jay*

Q. What is that blue bird with the pointed head?

A. Park visitors are impressed by the raucous and beautiful Steller's jay, which lives from the park's lowest elevations to the mixed conifer belt. Often called blue jays this species lacks the white markings

---

*The peregrine falcon nests on Yosemite's cliffs, and barn owls have nested in old barns here during past years. Both are found on all continents except Antarctica.*

of its eastern cousin. Also seen in the park are the western scrub jay in the lower elevations, and occasionally the pinyon jay in the high country.

Q. How many bird species found in the park are not native to Yosemite?
1) two    2) three    3) five
A. Among the five non-native birds that reside in the park, the wild turkey is the most recent addition. Native east of the Rocky Mountains, the turkey has spread from other parts of California where they were introduced. White-tailed ptarmigans were released in the Sierra Nevada east of the park in 1971 and 1972, and have spread throughout the high elevations of the park and up and down the Sierra. Brown-headed cowbirds, native to the Great Plains where they evolved with bison herds, followed livestock west and have increased in park areas where there are horse stables. Starlings were introduced into New York City's Central Park in the 1890s and spread across the continent. They are found in the lower elevations of the park, where they evict other birds from nesting cavities. House sparrows, though not common, are also sighted at the park's lower elevations.

Q. What are some of the rarest bird species sightings in the park?
A. A greater roadrunner was seen in Yosemite Valley in 1924. A yellow rail was sighted in Tuolumne Meadows in 1980 and none of these diminutive rails had been seen anywhere in California for the previous fifty years. The only known park sighting of an eastern kingbird was in Tuolumne Meadows in 2002.

Q. Which species have become more common during the last few decades?
A. The common merganser, common raven, and lazuli bunting. Common mergansers increased greatly in numbers after the flood of 1997. The population of common ravens (a carrion-eater) has risen with the increasing numbers of animals killed on park roads. More automobiles, driving at faster speeds, are the cause of a major food source for ravens. Lazuli bunting numbers rose in mid-elevation burn areas where new shrubs replaced dense forests.

---

*Great gray owls have a wingspan of five feet.*

**Q.** How many owl species have been seen in Yosemite?
1) seven   2) eleven   3) twelve
**A.** Yosemite's eleven species of owl represent more than half the owl species seen in the western United States. In comparison, both Mt. Rainier and Everglades national parks have six species of owl.

**Q.** What rare owl does the park provide essential habitat for?
**A.** Sixty-five percent of the California population of great gray owls (150) reside in the park, where important meadow habitat is protected from grazing and essential forest nesting sites are not logged. One danger to these magnificent owls is aggressive searching by bird watchers intent on seeing them. It is recommended that those interested in seeing great gray owls in the park look for them in an unobtrusive manner, especially during breeding season.

**Q.** In 2010 what discovery was made about Yosemite's great gray owls?
**A.** Recent genetic research determined that they are a genetically distinct population and placed them in a new subspecies, *Strix nebulosa yosemitensis*. This unique population is also evidenced by behavioral differences from other populations of great gray owls, showing that Yosemite's owls have been isolated from other populations for a long period of time.

*Great gray owl*

**Q.** How many duck species have been seen in Yosemite?
1) nine   2) twelve   3) nineteen
**A.** Yosemite's nineteen species of ducks is low compared to the twenty-eight species in Yellowstone and Everglades' thirty-one.

**Q.** Which common Yosemite woodpecker is also found in South America?
1) hairy   2) acorn   3) white-headed
**A.** Acorn woodpeckers are commonly seen nesting and feeding in Yosemite's California black oak groves. In Colombia, they may

---

*Yosemite is a woodpecker paradise, with 12 species, compared to Everglades National Park's 10, Glacier National Park's 11, and Isle Royale National Park's 8.*

be seen doing the same activities in mountains where there are groves of Humbolt oaks.

Q. Which summer-resident park birds can winter as far south as Argentina?
A. Cliff and barn swallows. When Wilson's phalaropes sometimes stop in the Yosemite high country during migration, they are on their way to the open grasslands and wetlands of Argentina.

Q. A white throated swift can fly as fast as
1) 200 mph    2) 160 mph    3) 175 mph
A. In diving, swifts can reach a speed of 160 mph, making them one of the fastest animals on the planet. Big-wall climbers often experience these jet-like birds zooming past them and sometimes witness swifts zipping at high speeds into the large cracks where they nest.

Q. The main prey species for the peregrine falcon are
1) hummingbirds    2) band-tailed pigeons
3) white-throated swifts
A. Peregrines kill both band-tailed pigeons and white-throated swifts, by striking them in the air.

Q. What was John Muir's favorite bird?
A. The American dipper, which he called the water ouzel, is a songbird that swims and walks under water as it hunts for aquatic insects and fish eggs. They have goggle-like membranes that cover their eyes while underwater, as well as oil glands to protect their feathers. Dipper nests are moss-covered domes often built within waterfall spray.

American dipper

Q. Which seabird commonly seen fishing along the ocean shores was found near the Mount Lyell Glacier?
A. In 1961, white pelican bones were discovered at 12,000 feet on a moraine at the eastern end of the glacial basin. White pelicans

---

*Peregrine falcons are the fastest creatures on the planet—
while diving, they can fly 175 mph.*

can sometimes be seen flying over the park as they migrate from the Central Valley and the Pacific Ocean to nesting sites in the Great Basin. Rufous hummingbirds have also been witnessed crossing over high peaks and passes.

Q. What bird has become rarer in the park during the last few decades?
A. Willow flycatchers nest in mid-elevation mountain meadows. They left lower-elevation meadows in the Sierra Nevada due to damage caused by livestock and changes in hydrology from roads, logging, fire suppression, mining, water diversions and climate change that have caused meadows to become drier. In 2007, park scientists concluded that willow flycatchers no longer nest in park meadows.

## Amphibians

Q. How many amphibian species live in the park?
1) seven    2) twelve    3) fourteen
A. Among these twelve species, six are salamanders, two are toads, and four are frogs. The most colorful of the salamanders, the Sierra newt, has a poison that is powerful enough to kill any predator that ingests them. Its bright-orange color is a warning to any animal that might consider it for dinner.

Q. Which amphibian is named after Yosemite?
A. The Yosemite toad. The female is larger than the male, which may be seen riding her piggyback during breeding season. The population of these toads has been in decline for the last quarter century.

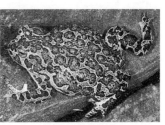
Yosemite toad

Q. Since these toads have poison glands, do any critters eat them?
A. Clark's nutcrackers eat the toads by flipping them over and pecking at their belly side, leaving the poison glands of the back untouched. Dragonfly nymphs and predaceous diving beetle larvae eat the tadpoles.

---

*Willow flycatchers have disappeared from the Yosemite Valley since 1966 because of the drying climate and other environmental changes.*

Q. Which frog species introduced to Yosemite is a threat to the survival of other frogs?
A. The bull frog is a voracious predator that eats the tadpoles of other frog species. Its native range is east of the Rocky Mountains.

Q. What is the amphibian that visitors are most likely to see in the park?
A. The Pacific tree frog, also known as the Pacific chorus frog, is more often found in meadows, in water or on rocks, than on trees. It is easily identified by its distinctive black eye mask and toe pads. Its tadpoles, which may hatch in temporary pools or ponds, can accelerate their development into frogs as the water disappears. These prematurely adult frogs may be as small as a fingernail.

Q. Does Yellowstone have more amphibian species than Yosemite?
A. No. It only has four, while Olympic National Park has thirteen.

Q. Which amphibian is named after the park's highest peak?
A. The Mount Lyell salamander was accidentally collected

*Mount Lyell salamander*

in a mousetrap in 1915 by the University of California Museum of Vertebrate Zoology survey team led by Professor Joseph Grinnell. The Mount Lyell salamander was the second species of web-toed salamander found in North America. The first, the Mount Shasta salamander, had been discovered in the early 1900s, but had not been officially described by scientists.

Q. When were additional species of web-toed salamanders discovered in California?
A. In 1952, the limestone salamander was found by herpetologist Joe Gorman in the Merced River Canyon east of the park and is only known to live in that area. A year later, Gorman re-discovered the Shasta salamander and confirmed that it was also a web-toed salamander. Finally, in the 1980s, another population of the Mount

*Before the Mount Lyell salamander was discovered, the only known species of its group had been seen in the mountains of the Italian and French Riviera.*

Lyell salamander was found in California's Owens Valley on the east side of the Sierra Nevada. Some scientists believe that this may actually be a new species.

**Q.** Camping is prohibited on Half Dome in to protect which amphibian?
**A.** Since 1992, camping has not been permitted atop Half Dome because of disturbing Mount Lyell salamanders and destruction of the few trees that grow there by firewood gathering.

## Reptiles

**Q.** How many reptile species live in Yosemite?
1) 8    2) 17    3) 22
**A.** 3) Of the twenty-two species living in the park, thirteen are snakes and eight are lizards.

**Q.** Is it legal to kill a rattlesnake in the park?
**A.** It is illegal to kill any animal in Yosemite. The majority of rattlesnake bites in the United States occur when *people* are at-
tacking the snakes. Rattlers routinely move out of the way if they are not pestered. When they rattle their tails, it is a warning to back off. The poison is used to kill small prey, such as mice. The similar-looking gopher snake lacks a rattle on its tail, but will sometime imitate a rattler to scare off predators.

*Rattlesnake*

**Q.** Which park snake looks like the venomous coral snake found in southern parts of the United States?
**A.** The seldom-seen mountain king snake has alternating rings of red, white and black, while a coral snake usually has yellow rings as well. King snakes are not venomous. The western king snake is known to attack and eat rattlesnakes.

**Q.** Are there boas in the park?
**A.** Yes. The rubber boa is related to larger boas, but rarely exceeds 2½ feet in length.

---

*Western rattlesnakes are the park's only poisonous snake species.*
*They're found mostly at lower elevations, but*
*have been encountered above 8,000'.*

Q. Is Yosemite home to turtles?
A. The only turtle species that inhabits the park is the western pond turtle. They live in slow-moving streams and ponds and may nest over 500 feet from water.

Q. Are there alligators in the park?
A. No, but you could see two species of alligator lizards. The larger of the two, the southern alligator lizard, can be up to a foot long. The western whiptail lizard, also a park resident, is even longer at fourteen inches.

Q. Do any lizards have blue tails?
A. The Gilbert's skink, a type of smooth skinned lizard, has a blue tail when it is young. This color is a lifesaver for these lizards. Predators can easily see the blue color and make a grab at the tail instead of the skink's head. The skink loses its tail, but escapes to safety. Like all lizards it can regrow the tail. As adults, skinks have orange heads and green bodies.

## Fish

Q. How many native fish species live in Yosemite National Park?
1) three    2) six    3) eleven
A. 2) The six natives are rainbow trout, California roach, Sacramento pike minnow, hardhead (a California species of concern), Sacramento sucker and riffle sculpin.

Q. In the 1860s the Whitney Survey did not find any fish in the Yosemite high country. What was their theory about the absence of fish from high-elevation lakes and streams?
A. They believed the water did not have enough oxygen.

Q. Where they right?
A. Not at all! Fish were probably resident in lakes and streams above Hetch Hetchy, Yosemite Valley, and the Wawona basin before the beginning of the ice ages three million years ago. Immense glaciers flowing down through the Merced and Tuolumne river watersheds scoured away all aquatic life in their path. When the glaciers receded they left behind steep canyons and hanging valleys, creating waterfalls and cascades along the main rivers

---

*When rattlers attack a larger animal, such as a human,*
*they often refrain from injecting poison.*

and their tributaries. Fish from the lower, unglaciated zones could not repopulate the higher areas because they couldn't make it upstream.

Q. When were non-native fish introduced to the park?
A. In 1877 rainbow trout were planted north of Hetch Hetchy. In 1893 eastern brook trout were planted in both the Tuolumne and Merced rivers. Rainbow trout is native on the lower Merced River, but is not native at the higher elevations. From 1877 to 1991 an estimated 33 million fish were stocked in the park.

*Rainbow trout*

Q. How many non-native fish species were introduced to the park through planting?
1) three   2) six   3) ten
A. These 10 are smallmouth bass, arctic grayling, brook trout, Dolly Varden, brown trout, Lahontan cutthroat trout (federally listed as threatened), Paiute cutthroat trout (threatened), golden trout, rainbow trout, and rainbow-golden hybrid trout.

Q. Of these ten how many are thought to no longer be surviving in the park?
1) one   2) three   3) six
A. Arctic grayling, Dolly Varden and Paiute cutthroat trout.

Q. Is a license needed to fish in Yosemite?
A. Yes, a California fishing license is required for anyone sixteen years of age or older. When the Yosemite Grant was transferred back to the federal government in 1905, it was agreed that California would have a right to require fishing licenses.

Q. Are there any other fishing regulations special to the park?
A. Yes, no live or dead minnows or other bait fish, amphibians, non-preserved fish eggs, or roe may be used or possessed. Fishing

---

*"Anadromous" fish are born in freshwater, and then go downstream to spend a year or two in the ocean before returning to their home streams to spawn.*

from bridges and docks is not allowed. Rainbow trout are catch-and-release only. Only artificial lures or flies with barbless hooks may be used, and bait fishing is prohibited. There are also seasonal restrictions for different areas of the park.

Q. Which native fish haven't been seen in the park since the late 1870s?
1) pike    2) chinook salmon    3) steelhead trout
A. 2) & 3) Historically there were both spring and fall salmon runs on the Merced River. Chinook salmon are thought to have been

abundant on the lower Merced River up to El Portal and slightly past the present park boundary. Above this section the river gradient increases to one too steep for chinook to ascend. However, it is thought that steelhead trout inhabited the river all the way up to Yosemite Valley. Steelhead trout are a variety of rainbow trout that

*Chinook salmon*

migrate to saltwater and return to freshwater to spawn.

Q. Why did the chinook salmon and steelhead trout disappear from the park?
A. They weren't able to make it past dams built on the lower portions of the Merced River.

Q. Where there ever fish hatcheries in the park?
A. Yes. In 1894 the state of California built a hatchery in Wawona, and in 1927 the state fish and game commission opened a hatchery at Happy Isles.

Q. Are there still hatcheries in the park?
A. No. Wawona fish hatchery was closed in 1914 due to the high summer water temperatures. Happy Isles hatchery was shut down in 1956 because of the high cost of operation. The current nature center at Happy Isles occupies one of the hatchery structures.

---

*Three dams on the Merced River, downstream and outside of Yosemite National Park, affect the fish species to be found in the park.*

Q. When did the Park Service stop stocking fish?
1) 1968    2) 1981    3) 1991
A. In 1991 the park ended that activity started over one hundred years before.

Q. What was the reason for this change in policy?
A. The National Park Service determined in the 1960s that they needed to protect the species present in the park at the time of their discovery by Euro-Americans. Biologists realized that fish populations in areas where they had not occurred historically adversely affected other life in the lakes, streams, and rivers. Park amphibians such as the Sierra Nevada yellow-legged frog have dropped dramatically, up to 95%, primarily due to predation by non-native fish.

Q. Did halting fish stocking reverse the impacts of non-native fish?
A. No, most of the populations of stocked fish continue to reproduce and survive without stocking.

Q. Is anything being done to restore amphibian populations?
A. Yes. In 2007, National Park Service biologists started a four-year experimental program to remove fish from eight lakes in the park backcountry.

Q. Are there other reasons why the Sierra Nevada yellow-legged frog populations have declined?
A. In 1999 a disease caused by amphibian chytrid fungus was identified. This pathogen has had a devastating impact on the frogs. Fortunately, some populations of Sierra Nevada yellow-legged frogs in the park are surviving despite the presence of this fungus.

## Insects and Other Invertebrates

Q. How many species of insects and other invertebrates are there in Yosemite?
A. There are perhaps thousands, but no comprehensive survey has been done

*Pseoduoscorpion*

---

*The Crocker-Huffman Diversion Dam (built 1907) completely blocked chinook salmon and steelhead trout from spawning in the Merced River headwaters in Yosemite.*

yet. In 2009, researchers searching for invertebrate species in park caves discovered a new species of psuedoscorpion (*Parabosum yosemitae*) in a cave frequented by park visitors. Doubtless there are numerous other invertebrate species unique to Yosemite yet to be discovered.

Q. What rare gastropod is found in Yosemite?
1) alpine slug    2) Yosemite sideband snail    3) Mirror Lake clam
A. 2) The Yosemite sideband snail lives in talus slopes near the Merced River.

Q. Is that a leech on your leg?
A. If you wade in a pond, you might discover tiny leeches on your legs when you return to shore. Though uncommon, leeches do live in a few park ponds. Some species primarily feed on snails, others on frogs, and others on aquatic invertebrates.

*Leeches*

These little bloodsuckers are easy to remove and don't transmit diseases to humans.

Q. Are there ticks in the park?

*Tick on a blade of grass*

A. Ticks live on rodents, deer and other park animals. Though they are not commonly picked up on walks, it is a good idea to check for ticks after hiking. The western black-legged tick, which occurs in Yosemite, is known to transmit Lyme disease. Relapsing fever (borelliosis), another tick-borne disease, is not common, but has been caught by people camping in the park's high country.

Q. What insect species was the first to be discovered in the park and have Yosemite as its species name?
A. On a June day in 1876, Baron Von Osten Sacken, an entomologist and Russian Consul General to the United States, collected three midges flying near the Yosemite Falls Trail close to the base of the upper falls. They turned out to be new to science and so he

---

*A tiny rice-grain-sized clam, called the ubiquitous clam, resides in Yosemite ponds, springs and slow-moving streams at elevations up to 8,600 feet.*

named them *Blepharocera yosemite* (Yosemite net winged midge). The nymphs of these midges live in fast moving streams and some species actually live on rock cliffs by or behind waterfalls.

Q. Since that time, which other insects have been discovered in the park and given "Yosemite" as their species name?
A. In 1925 James G. Needham, a professor at Cornell, one of the most prominent aquatic biologists of his time, and fellow professor Peter Claassen discovered and named a new species of stonefly (*Arcynopteryx yosemite*).

In 1946, C.P. Alexander, a crane fly expert and ex-student of Needham, collected the Yosemite crane fly (Tipula yosemite).

Since that time the Yosemite mayfly, Yosemite bark beetle, Yosemite shore fly and Yosemite shieldback grasshopper have all been found in the park.

Q. Which beetle flies up into the mountains in fall to overwinter?
1) ground beetles    2) stink beetles    3) ladybird beetles
A. 3) Convergent ladybird beetles, known more commonly as ladybugs, feed on aphids and scale insects in the Central Valley and foothills. In fall they fly to mid-elevation forests in the Sierra. They can be found on rocks or logs in large bright orange-red masses where they will stay dormant for the winter. In spring they fly downslope once more.

Q. Are there biting flies in Yosemite?
A. Deer flies and horse flies break the skin with their rasp-like teeth, causing a painful "bite." The gray colored snipe fly found at higher elevations in July also feeds on blood.

Q. Are there mosquitoes in the park?
A. May and early June are normally mosquito season in Yosemite Valley and Wawona. At higher elevations, mosquitoes emerge in late June through July.

Q. What are "snow" mosquitoes?
A. A small black mosquito (*Aedes ventrovittus*) is often called the snow mosquito because it appears at high elevation as snows are melting in mountain meadows. Their eggs, which have been

---

*Fairy shrimp, half-inch-long freshwater shrimp, may be found swimming upside down in Yosemite pools and ponds as high as 12,800' elevation.*

lying dormant in the meadows, hatch in the shallow snowmelt pools. These mosquitoes can appear in such vast numbers that they form black clouds and it's hard not to swallow them if your mouth is open. Fortunately for hikers, snow mosquitoes do not last for more than a week or two in any one location.

Q. Do both male and female mosquitoes bite?
A. Only the female bites because she needs blood to develop her eggs. Males are the pollinators, who visit long-spurred flowers including some orchid species.

Q. Which bees are not native to the park?
1) bumblebees   2) leaf cutter bees   3) honeybees
A. 3) Honeybees were introduced from Europe and are not significant pollinators of park flowers. There are many of families of solitary bees that lay their eggs on balls of pollen stashed in small burrows.

Q. Which common bee-like insect is a major pollinator of deep-throated flowers?
A. Bee flies are true flies that resemble bees because they are also fuzzy and have similar coloration. Unlike bees they have only two wings and can hover like hummingbirds. Adults of some species of bee flies lay eggs near the entrances to wild bee nests and their larvae feed on pollen stores and on bee larvae. The larvae of other species feed on cutworms, tiger beetle and sawfly larvae, and grasshopper eggs.

Q. What are those big blue black bees buzzing about in the forest?
A. Carpenter bees excavate colonies in wood, creating channels up to a foot long. Eggs are

*A carpenter bee and its colony*

provided with a honey/pollen mixture and after two months a new generation of adults emerges.

---

*Friendly little ladybugs actually do bite people—*
*they nip only when they're migrating.*

**Q.** What is the main pollinator in the higher elevations of the park?
1) monarch butterfly    2) hover fly    3) bumblebee
**A.** 3) Bumblebees are the predominant high-elevation pollinators because of their ability to pollinate at cool temperatures by regulating their own body temperature.

**Q.** Which butterflies overwinter as adults in the park?
1) California tortoiseshell    2) painted lady    3) monarch
**A.** The California tortoiseshell lays its eggs on wild lilacs and, during some years, there are flights of vast numbers of the newly hatched butterflies at the park boundary near El Portal.

**Q.** How many butterfly species have been observed in Yosemite National Park?
1) 67    2) 88    3) 109
**A.** At least 88 species have been seen in the park.

**Q.** Which butterflies species were first described from specimens collected in the park?
**A.** Sierra Nevada parnassian (*Parnassius behrii*) on Mount Lyell and Sierra Nevada blue (*Agriades podarce*) at the headwaters of the Tuolumne River.

**Q.** What is the lifespan of butterflies that live exclusively in the alpine zone of Yosemite?
**A.** Two to four weeks as adults.

**Q.** How long do alpine butterflies stay in their caterpillar phase?
**A.** Most of them live a year in the larval stage and survive the winter under snows in an inactive mode called diapause.

**Q.** Are alpine butterflies in Yosemite threatened?
**A.** Since they exist in small populations and limited habitats, they are sensitive to change. Studies show that some species are not found in locations where they were sighted from 1930 to 1960, and some are found in the same places, but with numbers diminished.

---

*Metallic wood borers and long horned beetles (common in Yosemite) start life eating the wood of dead or dying trees, and emerge as adults to feed on pollen in flowers such as mariposa lilies.*

Q. Which moth is an important pollinator at high elevations?
1) tussock moth    2) sphinx moth    3) giant silk moth
A. 2) Sphinx moths, also called hummingbird moths, pollinate alpine columbine and other deep-throated alpine flowers. Like bumblebees they are able to fly in cool weather because they can regulate their body temperatures by vibrating their wing muscles.

Q. Are there fireflies in Yosemite?
A. No, but glow worms live in the lower elevations of the park. These beetles are in the same family as fireflies. Only females, who remain in their wingless larval-like form, produce a greenish glow aimed at attracting the winged males.

Q. Which of these is adapted to living in or on snow?
1) wolf spider    2) springtail    3) scorpion fly
A. All of the above are active on snow in winter. Wolf spiders

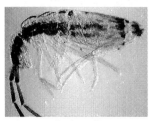

*Springtail*

may be found hunting on winter snows or high-elevation summer snowfields. They catch lower-elevation insects that are caught in air currents and then are deposited in snow where they become chilled and thus easy to catch. Springtails, or *collembola*, are called snow fleas when they are found on snow. As their name implies they can spring or hop like fleas as they search for pollen grains and fungal spores. Scorpionflies can be seen walking on the snow surface in winter. They feed on animal droppings

Q. What seldom-seen Yosemite insect lives exclusively on snow and on talus slopes?
A. Ice crawlers are extremely rare insects that require cool temperatures. Being held in a warm hand can be fatal! There are only 26 species of these wingless members of these cricket-like insects in the world. Entomologists have found them on the south side of Yosemite Valley and along the rim at Glacier Point.

Q. Which moth was thought to be a pest but is now known to play an important role in the health of the forest?

---

*Yosemite's 88 species of butterflies are far fewer than those in Grand Canyon National Park (four times as many) and Great Smoky Mountains National Park (seven times as many).*

1) plume moth   2) gypsy moth   3) lodgepole needleminer moth

A. 3) The lodgepole needleminer moth got a bad rap until its role in forest ecology became understood in recent years.

The *lodgepole needleminer moth* is primarily found in Sierra Nevada lodgepole pine forests. The caterpillar eats out the needles from the inside, hence its name needleminer. Over a period of two summers one of them mines out three to five needles. In mid-July of their second year they emerge from their cocoons as adult moths, mate, and lay eggs at the base of lodgepole pine needles.

The populations of these moths gradually build up over two or more decades. When the population nears its peak there are so many mined-out pine needles that a forest may appear to be dying. Evidence of past peak populations is the use of the name "tamarack" for lodgepole pines by 19th century settlers and loggers. Tamaracks, also known as larches, are conifers that grow in northern zones and shed their needles each year. Most likely the name, tamarack, was given by people who thought lodgepole pines were tamarack trees because they looked like they were shedding their needles as true tamaracks do.

In the late 1950s the National Park Service became concerned about the high populations of needleminer moths in lodgepole forests in Tuolumne Meadows, around Tenaya Lake, and along the Glacier Point Road. They were unaware that the moth and lodgepole pines had co-existed for millennia and that the open appearance of lodgepole forests in the Sierra resulted from this relationship. Because of this misunderstanding, the Park Service sprayed the forest with DDT and, in the early 1960s, with malathion.

The pesticide killed off the moth's predators and parasites, but not the all of the moths. Without their natural predators and parasites, the moth populations rebounded. Meanwhile, entomologists had realized that the needleminer moth was endemic to Sierran lodgepole forests and decided it did not pose a threat to the forests.

By the late 1970s the lodgepole forest in the Tuolumne Meadows basin appeared to be dying. The moth population

---

*Butterflies that live exclusively in Yosemite's alpine zone have a lifespan of two to four weeks as adults.*

reached a peak in the early 1980s and then dropped quickly due to the increase of parasites, predators, and other factors. Soon most of the forest was green again, except for stands of old weakened trees that couldn't withstand the defoliation.

In these high-elevation lodgepole pine forests, where summers are dry and growth is slow, fires are rare. There are simply not enough needles and woody debris on the ground to carry a fire. The lodgepole needleminer moth plays an important role in maintaining the overall health of such lodgepole pine forests, by keeping the forests open for new generations of trees to thrive.

Q. Are bark beetles killing trees in the park?

A. Newspapers often report that bark beetles are killing Sierra forests, but the beetles are only the final act in a long series of events.

Most of the forest ecosystems in the park are fire-adapted. This means that they survive light fires. Unfortunately, due to decades of fire suppression, most of these fire-adapted forests are now uncharacteristically dense and choked with fuel. Under these conditions, when a fire occurs—whether it is caused by humans or lightning—it can be devastating.

Besides the hazard of firestorms, the increase in forest density diminishes forest health because trees must compete more for light and water. Trees weakened by these conditions become susceptible to root diseases that spread from tree to tree. A healthy tree can repel bark beetles by flushing them out with sap.

Scientists have discovered that bark beetles can sense a chemical change in weakened trees and fly to them. In the process of feeding on these trees, the beetles introduce fungal spores as they bore into the trees to lay eggs. At this point, the trees die and open up the forest, but fuel levels are even higher and the forest is more apt to burn.

---

*Yosemite''s moisture-rich meadows make up only 3% of the park, but contain a much larger proportion of Yosemite's species—possibly 33%.*

## Wildlife Survival

Q. How does fire affect wildlife?

A. When naturally caused fires burn in chaparral, a plant community composed of thick-leaved shrubs, the fire-adapted shrubs re-sprout or re-seed creating extremely nutritious forage for deer and other wildlife. Frequent human-caused fire in this plant community will deplete seed stores and threaten survival.

*Crowded trees after a fire.*

In lower-elevation forests of oak, pine and incense cedar, low-intensity lightning fires will favor understory vegetation and oaks over conifers. This results in more food for wildlife.

The same is true for upper montane conifer forests, where understory shrubs and herbs all but disappear after years of fire suppression.

Q. When did the park start managing wildlife?

A. Before the establishment of the National Park Service, one of Yosemite's acting superintendents, Major Forsyth, thought that black bears were a danger to visitors and wrote to the U.S. Secretary of the Interior asking for permission to hunt bears out of the valley using shotguns loaded with small shot. In the early days of the park service, predators were thought of as a menace to other animals.

Mountain lions were considered the most harmful predator and a bounty was provided to encourage their extermination. Jay Bruce, "official cougar killer" for the State of California, was reported to have killed more than fifty cougars in or near the park from 1916 to 1919. Bruce boasted of having killed 669 mountain lions during his career.

Q. What did Bruce donate to the park?

A. In 1918 he donated three live mountain lion cubs to a small Yosemite Valley zoo that exhibited a caged bear and deer. Despite criticism about having caged animals, the zoo was not abolished until 1932.

---

*Today the National Park Service uses controlled fires called "prescribed burns" to help manage forest health.*

Q. When did the National Park Service start wildlife research?
1) 1919   2)   1923   3) 1928
A. George M. Wright, part of Yosemite's naturalist division, started research in the park in 1928 and soon oversaw projects in other parks as well. Wright realized that practices such as predator control upset the balance of wildlife populations. Later, other wildlife biologists promoted management based on ecological studies that showed that the health of prey populations, such as moose and deer, is dependent on their relationship to historic predators like wolves and mountain lions. Predators tend to catch old, deformed, injured, or diseased prey and thus, over time, contribute to a healthier prey population.

Q. How many mountains lions live in the park?
1) 10-20   2) 40-50   3) 60 or more
A. 2) A study in 2003 estimated one lion per 25 square miles, which means 40-50 lions might live in the park. Researchers tracked the whereabouts of 18 lions and discovered that many

*Mountain lions at their den*

of those inhabiting Yosemite roam outside the park boundaries. The park does not contain the wintering grounds of the park's deer and bighorn sheep, which are important prey of the lions.

Q. How many native animal species disappeared from the park by the early 1900s?
1) one   2) three   3) five
A. 3) Chinook salmon, Sierra bighorn sheep and the California grizzly were early casualties of destructive activities by Euro-Americans, such as mining, grazing, and hunting.

Q. What park animal became extinct?
1) bighorn sheep   2) California grizzly bear   3) timber wolf
A. The California grizzly became extinct in all of its range when the last known wild grizzly was killed south of Yosemite in 1922. There is no evidence that timber wolves were historically present in the Sierra Nevada despite place names such as White Wolf.

---

*The three park mammals endemic to the Sierra Nevada are: the Mount Lyell shrew, alpine chipmunk and long-eared chipmunk. Subspecies are the Sierra red fox and bighorn sheep.*

**Q.** What is the only park mammal listed as federally endangered under the Endangered Species Act?
1) bighorn sheep   2) wolverine   3) timber wolf
**A.** 1) The bighorn sheep was added to the endangered species list in the year 2000.

**Q.** Which park animal was re-introduced?
**A.** In 1986, twenty-seven bighorn sheep were brought from in a herd in the southern Sierra near Mt. Baxter and were released into

*Bighorn sheep*

the Lee Vining Canyon area outside the park's eastern border. Two years later, eleven more bighorns were released and, by 1994, the population in and near Yosemite increased to almost 100. As a result of harsh winters during the following years, about 60% of the herd died, and this decline continued until so few sheep existed in 1995 that scientists could recognize them as individuals. By 2001 the reproductive base of the local herd consisted of three separate female groups, each with only two to three ewes. Nine years later, the Yosemite bighorn sheep consisted of only about 35 or 40 animals.

**Q.** What had to be done before the sheep could be released in the park?
**A.** With the help of private donors the Yosemite Association paid a sheepherder to give up his grazing allotment in Lee Vining Canyon, so the bighorns would descend for their winter range. If domestic sheep were present, the bighorns could get blue tongue, the disease that killed the park's original bighorn populations.

**Q.** How did biologists get these sheep to the park?
**A.** Yosemite's bighorn sheep arrived via helicopter.

**Q.** How many Yosemite species are federally listed as endangered?
1) one   2) two   3) five
**A.** 2) The valley elderberry longhorn beetle and Sierra Neva-

---

*The four endemic amphibians are the Sierra Nevada ensatina,
the Mount Lyell salamander, the Yosemite toad, and
the Sierra yellow-legged frog.*

da bighorn sheep. The California red legged frog is "threatened," or in less danger.

**Q.** Have Yosemite animals been impacted by climate change?
**A.** Since Joseph Grinnell and his team from the University of California Museum of Vertebrate Zoology studied animal life in the park over 90 years ago, more than half the small mammal species—such as shrews, chipmunks, ground squirrels, and mice—have moved upslope by at least 1,600'. The alpine chipmunk, once common in the Tenaya Lake area and Tuolumne Meadows, now is found only above 9,600'—a change of almost 2,000' in elevation. Birds such as the yellow warbler and lazuli bunting have also moved due to precipitation changes.

*Joseph Grinnell at work*

## *Puzzlers*
### QUOTE QUEST #4

*Find the underlined words in eight different directions from this quote by park naturalist Enid Michael from a newspaper article on park bears:* "He **floats** like a **barrel** and **turns** over on his **back**, all **four feet** held out of the **water**. Down the **middle** of the **stream** he **swims**, and his wake opens a **broad path** of **silver**. When he encounters a **shallow**, he **slaps** the water with his paw, gives a **great leap**, and falls back with a **mighty splash**." *When all the clues have been circled, the remaining letters will spell what humorist Will Rogers, said after visiting Yosemite Valley.*

---

*Yosemite bird species that the State of California lists as endangered are the willow flycatcher and great gray owl.*

```
T H E R E T A W Y W A R S
N Y S S T A E R G O U L N
O W I T T T O F F E A E D
T O L A P H E O B P E A R
S L V O B A U U S T T H E
M L E L Y S T R T U R N S
A A R F M H L H B R O A D
E H P I E E A Y V E A H O
R S W A R L T B S P F I T
T S A R E H D L A E F O R
S T A H G L O D E C S E T
H B A I T D O T I V K N N
V N M S P L A S H M H Z Y
```

*Hidden message*: "_ _ _ _

_ _ _ _  _ _ _  _ _ _  _ _  _ _ _ _  _ _ _  _ _ _ _ _  _ _ _

_ _ _ _  _ _ _ _  _  _ _ _ _ _ _ _ _

_ _ _  _ _ _ _ _  _ _ _ _  _ _."

## YOSEMITE WORD SCRAMBLE

Unscramble the letters to find names of Yosemite residents and places.

*Wildlife*
1. TARGE YGRA LOWl
2. APKI
3. EYOMIST DTAO
4. TOTPSDE  TBA
5. LEMU EERD
6. GNRATLIN TCA
7. FIPIACA SREFIH
8. KLABC FIWST
9. OIUAMNIT KANENGISK
10. CLAKB REBA
11. LLSEETSR YJA

*Things*
12. QAUEOIS
13. LAFAWLRET
14. FLFIC
15. DCROHI
16. RGAIELC
17. HKAEIWBRT IENP
18. DICOLERKS
19. TNNHGIILH

*Places*
20. MEUTOUELN
21. RACEGIL INTOP
22. LE TACPINA

---

*California lists the Sierra red fox and the wolverine as threatened.*

## QUOTE QUEST #5

*Find the underlined words in eight different directions from this quote by John Muir about his favorite bird, the ouzel or dipper, which he called a water thrush:* "In **form** he is **about** as **smoothly plump** and **compact** as a **pebble** that is been **whirled** in a pot-hole, the **flowing contour** of his body being **interrupted** by his **strong** feet and tail, **crisp wing tips**, and the **slanted wren**-like **tail**." *When all the clues have been circled, the remaining letters will spell what William Leon Dawson, author of Birds of California, said about one of Yosemite's fastest birds.*

```
D E T P U R R E T N I R
C S W D E L R I H W I U
O M T F T E R T H A N O
M R I S W T I P P F T T
P O P I U P S E L W T N
A F S O S G B H R U E O
C W B I H B N E L I M C
T A R T L E N I W I T P
H C R E O A T E W I A D
S M O O T H L Y S O N T
W I S L A N T E D F L G
T C S T R O N G F L Q F
```

Hidden message: "_ _ _ _ _ _ _   _ _ _ _   _ _ _ _ _   _ _   _ _ _

_ _ _ _ _   _ _ _ _ _ _ _ _   _ _ _ _ _"

## JOKES

Q. Where does a 300-pound bear picnic in Yosemite?
A. Wherever it wants to.

Q. Why do other Yosemite critters go to black bears for answers?
A. They have the bear facts.

Q. Which bug isn't allowed in the park?
A. A litterbug.

---

*Even though grizzly bears are extinct in California, the animal remains on the state flag.*

# PEOPLE ON THE LAND

Q. The Native American name for Yosemite Valley is
1) Hetch Hetchy    2) Illilouette    3) Ahwahnee
A. 3) *Ahwahnee*, which means "place of gaping mouth," is the original name for the valley.

Q. The first people called themselves the
1) Ahwahneechee    2) Yosemite    3) Chowchilla    4) Yokut
A. 1) "Ahwahneechee," which means the "people of Ahwahnee."

Q. The Ahwahneechee lived in Yosemite continuously before the invasion of white people.
1) True    **2) False**
A. 2) That's false. They left around 1780, perhaps due to a smallpox outbreak, and joined the Mono Paiute on the eastern side of the Sierra. Forty to fifty years later, about 200 people returned with Tenaya, their chief. Tenaya's father was an Ahwahneechee and his mother a Mono Paiute. It is said that a medicine man told Tenaya the sickness was gone and that it was safe to return to their ancestral home.

**What happened around two decades after the Ahwahneechee returned to Ahwahnee?**

From the beginning of the California gold rush, there were conflicts between the Indians and miners. So many miners came into the mountains that, within a few years, vast areas were deforested and deer herds greatly diminished.

In the fall of 1850, the Ahwahneechee attacked a trading post belonging to James Savage, at the lower Merced River's confluence with its South Fork. Other Native American groups in gold mining country were also making raids on miners and trading posts. The miners asked for protection from the United States government, which responded by sending Indian commissioners. These officials demanded that the Ahwahneechee and six other tribes move onto a reservation.

In early 1851 all the tribes except the Ahwahneechee gathered at a military camp outside Agua Fria to make a treaty. Chief Tenaya arrived late and stated that he did not want to go to a reservation. On March 27, 1851, the Mariposa Battalion, a force of fifty-seven soldiers commissioned by the governor of California and led by James Savage (commissioned a major), entered Yosemite Valley in pursuit of the Ahwahneechee. They found only a few elders, who were not able to flee. All the rest had escaped. Soldiers destroyed shelters and stores of acorns and other crucial foods. Then it returned to Agua Fria.

In May, under the leadership Captain John Boling, the Mariposa Battalion returned to Yosemite and caught Tenaya and his band at a high-country lake known as Pywiack, "the lake of the shining rocks." It was renamed Lake Tenaya by the soldiers. On a forced march, the Ahwahneechee were taken to the Fresno Reservation. That winter some of the Ahwahneechee returned home to their valley.

Q. Where did the name Yosemite come from?
A. It is thought that Yosemite comes from the Miwok Indian word "Yohemite," which means "those who kill" or "some of them are killers." Tenaya and his fellow Ahwahneechee spoke Paiute.

---

*Archeological evidence, such as obsidian flakes from tool-making, shows that people have been living in Yosemite Valley for over 4,000 years.*

Lafayette Bunnell, a member of the Mariposa Battalion, suggested that the Valley be named "Yosemity," not knowing that Ahwahn-eechees' name for the valley was Ahwahnee, and that Yohemite was a name other Indians used for the Ahwahneechee.

Maria Lebrado, who was a child at the time the soldiers came in 1851, said in a 1928 interview that the other Indians who had made treaties with the government were enemies of the Ahwahneechee.

*Tredwell Moore*

Q. Did conflicts continue?

A. Yes. In May of 1852, two prospectors were killed in an attack near Bridalveil Meadow. A group of U.S. infantry commanded by Lt. Tredwell Moore entered Yosemite in June and killed several Indians, but didn't catch Tenaya and his main band. In 1853 Tenaya and his band returned to the valley, where he was killed by another tribe whose horse he and his band had stolen.

Q. Who was the first non-Indian to view Yosemite Valley?

A. It is thought that explorer Joseph Walker may have seen the valley from its rim as he was crossing the Sierra in 1833.

Q. Within two years of the death of Chief Tenaya what major event occurred?

A. In 1855, James Hutchings brought the first tourist group to Yosemite Valley. With him was the artist Thomas Ayres, who sketched the sights. When Hutchings published lithographs of Ayres' drawings, these provide the first pictorial glimpse of Yosemite to the outside world.

Q. When was the first toll trail built to the Yosemite Valley?

A. In 1856, Andrew, Huston, and Milton Mann completed a horse trail from Mormon Bar, near the town of Mariposa, to Yosemite Valley via present-day Wawona. The round-trip charge was $4 per horse or wagon or $2 for walkers. That same year, George Coulter and Lafayette Bunnell built Coulterville Free Trail, which passed by Hazel Green, Crane Flat, and Tamarack Flat.

---

*In 1855, the Yosemite Valley had a total of 32 visitors.*

**Q.** When was the first lodging constructed in the valley?
**A.** That same year of 1856, Hite and Walworth constructed the Lower Hotel near the base of Sentinel Rock. Two years later Mr. and Mrs. John Neals built the Upper Hotel.

**Q.** Did the Ahwahneechee people continue to live in Yosemite Valley after the coming of tourists?
**A.** In the 1850s, only a small number of them lived there year round. In 1857 a large group came to the valley to harvest an exceptionally bountiful acorn crop. Through the 1860s they continued to live in the valley, harvesting acorns and burning areas as they had for centuries, to make the oaks more productive and to improve growth of shrubs used for making baskets, arrow shafts, and other items. As the number of tourists increased with the opening of roads to Yosemite Valley, so did work opportunities. The valley's Indian population increased, as families living in other areas returned.

**Q.** What kind of work did they do?
**A.** Men worked for hotel owners putting up hay, chopping wood, and driving wagons. They also provided fish and game for tourists, in addition to serving as guides. Women worked as housekeepers in the homes of hotel owners and labored as maids and laundresses in the lodgings.

**Q.** Who blazed a trail around 1857 from Big Oak Flat to Mono Lake, which incorporated some of the historic Mono Trail used by Paiutes?
1) John Conway   2) Tom McGee   3) Theodore Solomons
**A.** 2) Tom McGee, a pack operator and saloonkeeper, blazed this route, some of it following trails used by the Ahwahneechee. This same year Galen Clark settled on South Fork of the Merced at present-day Wawona and named his place Clark's Station. Clark and Milton Mann visited the Mariposa Grove of Big Trees for the first time, and later started guiding tourists there.

**Q.** Who was the first year-round non-Indian resident in Yosemite Valley?
**A.** James C. Lamon took up a pre-emption claim in the valley's

---

*The town of Yosemite, Kentucky, was established in the 1870s for logging operations by businessman Eugene Zimmerman and named by his daughter. Locals pronounce it "Yo-seh-mite."*

upper end in the fall of 1859, built the first log cabin in Yosemite Valley, and laid out a garden and orchard. From the winter of 1861-62, he lived here year-round until his death in 1875.

**Q.** In the midst of the Civil War, what remarkable action was made by Abraham Lincoln?

**A.** On June 30, 1864, Lincoln signed a congressional bill to protect Yosemite Valley and the Mariposa Grove of Big Trees from logging, grazing, and other destructive practices, granting them to the State of California as preserves. Thus Yosemite became the first park land set aside by the federal government for the purpose of preserving its wild condition. Galen Clark was appointed Yosemite's first guardian. That year visitation to the valley totaled 147 tourists.

*James Hutchings*

**Q.** Who took over the Upper Hotel this same year?

**A.** James Hutchings purchased the hotel and renamed it the Hutchings House. It normally accommodated twenty-eight guests, but at times hosted as many as fifty-seven. In August 1864, Hutchings' wife Elvira gave birth to the first non-Indian child born in Yosemite, their daughter Florence.

**Q.** Who was appointed as chairman of the commission to the new state reserve?

1) Galen Clark   2) Frederick Law Olmstead   3) James Hutchings

**A.** 2) Frederick Law Olmstead was co-designer of New York City's Central Park and had served as manager of John C. Fremont's gold-country estate, Las Mariposas. His report on the new reserve was one of the first public testimonies expressing the significance of wilderness areas and natural scenery for human well-being. He also recommended a management policy for human access to the park that would minimize impacts to the natural environment.

**Q.** When a young man arrived in San Francisco in March of 1868, he asked a passerby the closest way out of town. When asked in return where he wanted to go, the young man replied, "Anywhere

---

*Frederick Law Olmstead was co-designer of New York City's Central Park as well as a wildernesss preservationist.*

that is wild." He started south on foot and crossed the interior coastal range at Pacheco Pass, where he had his first view across the flowery Central Valley to the lofty snow-covered Sierra Nevada Mountains. He continued walking until he reached his destination, Yosemite Valley. Who was this young man?
1) Josiah Whitney   2) Grizzly Adams
3) John Muir

*John Muir*
*around age 40*

A. 3) Muir told this story of his arrival in San Francisco later in his life, when he was famous. Whether true or not, it fits the persona created in his writing and his life. There is no doubt that Muir walked to Yosemite and that it captivated him.

Q. What was Muir's job when he first lived in Yosemite Valley in the fall of 1869?
1) handyman   2) baker   3) cook
A. 1) Muir served as a handyman for Hutchings, a job that provided him with time to explore the mountains. He spent much time with the Hutchings and was particularly fond of their five-year-old tomboy daughter Florence, whom he nicknamed "Squirrel."

Q. What book was published that same year of 1869?
A. Josiah Whitney's State Geological Survey released the first edition of *The Yosemite Book.*

Q. Muir helped build and operate a sawmill for James Hutchings. This seems out of character with his later efforts to protect Yosemite from logging and other damaging activities. Was it?
A. As a young man, Muir demonstrated an inventive genius, creating and modifying machinery. He devised watermills, door locks, an automatic horse feeder and a bed that would dump its occupant out when it was time to get up in the morning. His most remarkable creations were clocks with all their parts carved from pine. In 1860 he earned praise and prizes at the Wisconsin State Fair for his inventions, as well as the opportunity to attend the state university. The Hutchings sawmill, which was built near

---

*"I am dead and gone to heaven."*
*—John Muir, on first viewing the Yosemite Valley.*

Yosemite Creek, had a waterwheel to power the saw, but only downed trees were milled with it.

**Q.** Including the Hutchings House, how many hotels were in Yosemite in 1869?
1) three    2) four    3) five
**A.** 3) Tourism was booming in the new state preserve by then, with a total of five hotels serving tourists in the Yosemite Valley. Annual visitation now exceeded 600.

**Q.** What famous writer visited Muir in Yosemite in 1871?
1) Mark Twain    2) Nathaniel Hawthorne    3) Ralph Waldo Emerson
**A.** Emerson was friends with Muir's mentors Ezra Carr, a professor at the newly created University of California, and with his wife Jeanne. When Muir heard that Emerson was going come to Yosemite for a short visit, he wrote the essayist saying that El Capitan and Tissiack demanded that he stay longer. During the visit Emerson was impressed by Muir's writings and life as a scholar, and also as a man of action. Muir, on the other hand, was disappointed by Emerson's traveling companions, Eastern devotees who would not let the elderly writer camp out among the big trees of the Mariposa Grove.

**Q.** When was a horseback trail built to the base of Nevada Fall?
**A.** 1870. That year, Mr. and Mrs. Albert Snow also opened La Casa Nevada near the foot of the falls, and the valley had 1,735 visitors.

**Q.** When did John Muir and his artist friend William Keith first meet?
**A.** In 1872, Keith arrived at Muir's

*La Casa Nevada*

Yosemite Valley cabin with a letter of introduction from friends in the San Francisco Bay Area. The two Scottish immigrants became lifelong friends and over the years tramped and camped together in the High Sierra. At times Muir stayed with Keith while in San Francisco.

---

*In the 1870s, John Conway built four toll trails: from La Casa Nevada to Little Yosemite Valley, Four Mile Trail at Glacier Point, to the top of Yosemite Falls, and also to Eagle Peak's summit.*

Q. In what year could you first travel into Yosemite Valley by stagecoach?
1) 1869   2) 1872   3) 1874
A. The Coulterville Yosemite Turnpike opened to traffic in June 1874, and the Old Big Oak Flat Road opened the next month. The following summer, wagons and stagecoaches traveled from Mariposa to Yosemite on the newly opened Mariposa/Wawona Road, which was built using Chinese labor.

Q. When did the first public campground open in Yosemite Valley?
A. In 1874 G.A. Harris leased Lamon's old homestead. There he grew fruit, strawberries, and vegetables that were sold to innkeepers and campers. In 1878 he opened a campground and is credited with having the first store in the valley.

*Yosemite Chapel*

Q. The oldest building still standing in Yosemite Valley was built in 1879. What is it?
1) the Sentinel Hotel outhouse
2) Yosemite Chapel   3) Lower Hotel
A. 2) It's the chapel that, despite damage over the years from flooding, still offers Sunday services and hosts a great number of weddings.

Q. Why was the old village site near the Yosemite Chapel abandoned?
A. There had been too much damage from flooding over the previous years.

Q. When were the first photographs of Yosemite Valley taken?
A. Photographer Charles Weeds was brought to Yosemite Valley by James Hutchings to make the first photographs in 1859. In September of that year his photographs were exhibited in San Francisco. From the very beginning, paintings, drawings, and photographs were used by businessmen such as James Hutchings to promote tourism to Yosemite.

---

*Campground keeper and market gardener G.A. Harris,*
*an observant Jew, had to order matzoh from a San Francisco*
*bakery for his Passover Seders.*

*Albert Bierstadt*

**Q.** Which well known artists camped for seven weeks in Yosemite in 1863?
**A.** Albert Bierstadt, Virgil Williams, and E.W. Perry visited the Yosemite Valley with writer Fitzhugh Ludlow.

**Q.** Which two painters had studios in Yosemite?
1) Albert Bierstadt    2) Chris Jorgenson
3) Thomas Hill
**A.** Thomas Hill became well known in the late 1870s for his paintings of Yosemite landscapes and built a studio in Wawona in 1884. During the summers of 1898 and 1889 Chris Jorgenson camped in Yosemite Valley. In 1900 he built his first cottage, a studio and residence, along the north bank of the Merced River.

**Q.** In 1880, who was appointed as the new guardian of the Yosemite Grant?
**A.** James Hutchings replaced Galen Clark. Nine years later, Clark became guardian again at the age of seventy-two.

**Q.** What two tragic deaths occurred in Yosemite Valley in 1881?
**A.** Florence Hutchings had grown up to be an adventurous young woman. She wore britches and tucked her long tresses under her hat while on horseback. When stagecoaches arrived in the valley, she would rear up on her horse, take off her hat, and shock the tourists who saw that she was a girl. Her best friend, Effie Crippen, was the daughter of a former Mariposa County sheriff and the stepdaughter of the manager of the Barnard Hotel.

*Flo Hutchings*

At the end of August 1881, while Effie and Florence were swimming at Mirror Lake, Effie stepped on broken glass. The bleeding was so severe that she died before they could get help. Less than a month later, while Florence was climbing the ledge trail to Glacier Point with friends, she was struck by a large rock. She was carried back to her cabin where she died the next day at the age of seventeen. The Yosemite Chapel organ was donated in her memory.

---

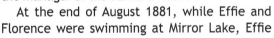

*When Sir Arthur Gilbert (of the Gilbert and Sullivan operetta duo) visited Yosemite in July 1885, he played the Chapel's organ for a memorial service for recently-deceased Ulysses S. Grant.*

Q. The first bakery opened in Yosemite Valley in 1884. Though it is no longer under the family's management, a restaurant and deli still bears their name. What was the family name?
1) Degnan   2) Curry   3) Leidig
A. 1) By the turn of the 20th century there was such a demand for bread that the Degnans purchased a large brick oven capable of baking more than 100 loaves of bread at a time. This oven is now part of the Pioneer History Center at Wawona.

Q. Who homesteaded 160 acres in Tuolumne Meadows in 1885?
1) James McCauley   2) James Hutchings
3) John Baptiste Lembert
A. 3) Lembert tried to raise goats, but they couldn't survive through the winter. His source of income became the sale of butterflies, captured in high-country forests and meadows, to collectors and museums.

Q. In the 1880s two new Yosemite roads were built. What were they?
A. The Glacier Point Road opened to stagecoach traffic in 1882, and the Great Sierra Wagon Road opened in 1883. The later road was built as a supply route for the Great Sierra Consolidated Mining

Company's operations on the eastern side of Tioga Pass. About 250 Chinese laborers worked for $1.50 apiece per day on road construction, which started in fall of 1882 and was completed the following September. In just 130 days, this 56-mile road was built across the Yosemite Sierra for a cost of $61,095. Shortly after its completion the mines closed and the road fell into disrepair.

*Yosemite stage station, now at Pioneer Yosemite History Center*

Q. After all these years of trail and road building, what did visitation climb to by 1884?
A. 4,000.

Q. Which Yosemite Lake was dammed in 1889 to prevent its transformation into a meadow?

---

*Photographer George Fiske was an apprentice to Charles Week, and also worked with Carleton Watkins.*

**A.** Mirror Lake, created when a rockfall dammed Tenaya Creek, began filling with silt. A dam was constructed to raise the lake level and, later, silt and sand were dredged from it for many years.

**Q.** Who teamed up with John Muir to advocate the creation of Yosemite National Park?
**A.** In the summer of 1889, while camped in Tuolumne Meadows, Robert Underwood Johnson and Muir came up with plans to lobby Congress to protect the greater Yosemite area, which included the headwaters of both the Tuolumne and Merced river watersheds. Johnson was editor of the influential *Century* magazine, where Muir began publishing articles about their plan. By October 1890, Congress created Yosemite National Park.

**Q.** When was Yosemite National Park established?
**A.** On September 30, 1890 President Harrison signed a bill making Yosemite the third national park. Yellowstone had been set aside in 1872, and Sequoia National Park became the second national park only six days before Yosemite. Three years after Yosemite's creation, Harrison set aside the 13-million-acre Sierra Forest Reserve, much of which bordered Yosemite National Park.

**Q.** How was the new national park protected from people who wanted to continue to use the area for hunting, grazing, logging, and mining?
**A.** The 4th Cavalry of U.S. Army was given the task of protecting the park, with Captain A. E. Wood in charge. Camp Wood, the headquarters, was located in Wawona. From 1891 to 1913, the cavalry patrolled the park each year (from mid-May to late fall). During this period, the park was supervised by ten successive army officers. Captain H.C. Benson and Major W.W. Forsyth both served four-year terms, the longest of any officers.

**Q.** Why was headquarters in Wawona and not Yosemite Valley?
**A.** Yosemite Valley and the Mariposa Grove were still under State of California control.

**Q.** Since grazing was no longer permitted in the area now protected within the park, what did the cavalry do to discourage

---

*Today, the Sierra Club has more than 1.4 million members.*

sheepherders from grazing their flocks in Yosemite?

A. They escorted them to the park boundary and left the sheep to scatter and be eaten by predators.

Q. What part of this historical period wasn't uncovered until many years later?

A. African-American troops of the 24th Infantry and 9th Cavalry, also known as "buffalo soldiers," patrolled the park in 1899, 1903, and 1904. Many of them were veterans of the Spanish American War. Though they wore the uniform of the U.S. cavalry that didn't stop them from being subjected to racist attitudes. This made their job of evicting shepherds, loggers, and hunters from Yosemite and Sequoia national parks very challenging. In addition they had to confiscate guns as well as build park roads, trails, and other infrastructure. Most of the commanding officers were Euro-Americans except for Charles Young, who served as acting superintendent of Sequoia National Park. Young, the third African-American graduate of the U.S. military academy at West Point, is considered to be the first black superintendent of a national park.

*24th Infantry soldiers patrolling Yosemite, 1899*

Q. Who patrolled the park in 1898 when troops were recalled to fight in the Spanish American War?

A. The General Land Office hired eleven men to patrol the park from June 25 until September 1, 1898. This first civilian ranger force was a success. In less than three months they expelled 189,000 head of sheep, 350 head of horses and 1,000 head of cattle from the park. In addition they confiscated 27 firearms. Among these first rangers were Archie Leonard and Charles Leidig. Leonard was assigned as scout and guide for the troops during the summer months. Leidig, the first Euro-American boy born in

---

*Plains Indians gave the "buffalo soldiers" their nickname, thinking that the men's curly hair look like the coats of bison.*

Yosemite Valley, worked with Leonard during winter, patrolling the park and enforcing regulations while the army troops were back at the Presidio in San Francisco.

Q. Which current entrance station locations were not in the original 1890 boundaries of the park?
1) Tioga Pass   2) Arch Rock   3) South Entrance
4) Big Oak Flat Entrance
A. Tioga Pass and the South Entrance did not become part of the park until later.

Q. When did Muir help establish the Sierra Club?
A. The club was established in June 1892. Muir was its first president, with Warren Olney, a lawyer who had hiked much of the Sierra, as vice president.

Q. How many people were charter members?
A. 182. Their common goal was "to explore, enjoy, and render accessible the mountain regions of the Pacific Coast; to publish authentic information concerning them," and "to enlist the support and cooperation of the people and government in preserving the forests and other natural features of the Sierra Nevada."

Q. Which famous geologist died in the park in 1901?
1) Clarence King   2) Joseph LeConte   3) Josiah Whitney
A. Professor Joseph LeConte died from a heart attack on the Sierra Club's first "High Trip," an annual summer outing for members held in the club's early days. He was 78 years old.

Q. In later years, which two lodges did the Sierra Club construct in the park?
A. In 1903 they built the LeConte Memorial Lodge in Yosemite Valley and in 1914 they began construction of Parsons Memorial Lodge in Tuolumne Meadows on land they had purchased from the McCauley family.

Q. Camp Curry was established in what year?
1) 1880   2) 1899   3) 1904

---

*When the U.S. Army experimented with bicycles for troop transport, the buffalo soldiers were among the units who tried out wheels.*

A. 2) Camp Curry got its start during the summer of 1899 with seven guest tents set up by David and Jennie Curry. An additional tent was used as kitchen and dining hall. Staff was Stanford University students who worked for room and board. It was the first lodging of this kind built in any national park. Later, with its wooden floored "tent cabins" and Adirondack-  style furniture, it developed a distinct rustic ambience. Following the opening of the Yosemite Valley Railroad less than ten years later, Camp Curry  became the main lodging in the valley.

Q. What offered a daily spectacle for guests of Curry Village?
A. The fire falls. In 1874 James McCauley conceived the idea of pushing burning embers off the cliff near his Mountain House lodging at Glacier Point as a way to advertise his accommodations. After Mc-Cauley's death, David Curry started up the fire falls again for special occasions, such as the presence of prominent guests at Camp Curry. It was so popular that it soon became a nightly event during sum-mer. A full-time employee was needed to gather the firewood, build a fire, and shove the coals off the cliff each night. Soon a special tradition arose. At precisely 9 P.M., before the coals were released, Mr. Curry would start the ceremony by calling out in his booming voice. "Hello, Glacier Point!" The fire maker would reply, "Are you ready, Camp Curry?" And then Mr. Curry would answer, "Let the fire fall!" High above from Glacier Point, bright embers slowly began to fall until becoming a blazing stream of red and gold shifting in the wind, with star-like sparks flying off into the air. Then the stream of glowing coals would become smaller and smaller until it was no more than a thin thread of gold.

Q. When and why did this tradition end?
A. By the early 1960s, the National Park Service decided that it was not a park service mission to allow man-made attractions. The fire falls ended in 1968. Traffic congestion, trampling of meadows by onlookers, rowdiness of the crowds, and burning excessive amounts of red fir bark were given as reasons for ending this unique spectacle.

-------------------

*By 1902 there were over 8,000 visitors a year to Yosemite Valley.*

Q. What is the oldest hotel in the park still in operation?
1) Yosemite Lodge    2) Wawona Hotel    3) Ahwahnee Hotel
A. 2) Clark Cottage was built in 1876 and is the oldest building in the present Wawona Hotel complex.

Q. Who was inspired as a boy by Carleton Watkins' photographs, and later in life became Yosemite's most famous photographer?
A. As a young boy Ansel Adams saw Watkins photos and switched from his goal of being a concert pianist to studying photography.

Q. Which photographer has a Yosemite landmark named for him?
A. Carleton Watkins, who provided photographs for the publications of the

*Ansel Adams*

Whitney Survey. In one of his early photographs of Mirror Lake, a part of Half Dome and another mountain are visible in the reflection. The second peak was later named Mt. Watkins. The very first photograph of a giant sequoia was taken by Watkins in the Mariposa Grove in the late 1850s. Watkins used a large-plate camera capable of taking 18" x 22" photographs. He used this camera in 1861 to capture his first images of Yosemite Valley. The resulting prints caused a sensation when they were shown in New York, and were used by Senator John Conness to convince Congress to enact the Yosemite Bill in 1864.

Q. Who was the first photographer to live in Yosemite Valley and photograph it through all the seasons?
1) Ansel Adams    2) Carleton Watkins    3) George Fiske
A. 3) In 1879, Fiske and his wife moved to Yosemite and lived here until he died in 1918. He was living alone and had become so despondent that he took his own life. Most of his negatives had been destroyed when his house burned in 1904.

Q. What famous photographer also began his career by assisting Watkins?
A. Eadweard Muybridge learned photography from Watkins and began his career photographing San Francisco and Yosemite. He

*The highest price paid so far for an Ansel Adams print is $722,000 for the mural-sized "Clearing Winter Storm."*

is best known for his photographs that capture the movement of people and animals. In 1879 he invented the Zoopraxiscope, the predecessor of the movie camera.

Q. Which former hotel owner and park guardian died from an accident in Yosemite in 1902?
A. James Hutchings was killed in a carriage accident on the old Big Oak Flat Road. He was 82 years old.

Q. Which other Yosemite pioneer died in a road accident a few years later?
A. James McCauley died in an accident on June 24, 1911 while driving a loaded wagon down the steep descent of the Coulterville Road into Yosemite Valley.

Q. What year did the first automobile drive into Yosemite Valley?
1) 1886    3) 1900    4) 1907
A. 3) On June 24, 1900, a Stanley steamer, driven by Oliver Lippincott, entered the valley via the Wawona Road.

Q. When were cars banned from roads going to Happy Isles and Mirror Lake?
A. On July 8, 1970, the Yosemite superintendent announced that Mirror Lake and Happy Isles would be closed to all vehicle traffic except that used for maintenance and medical emergencies, shuttle buses, and bicycles.

Q. When did the State of California transfer Yosemite Valley and Mariposa Grove to the federal government?
1) 1895    2) 1905    3) 1910    4) never
A. 2) In 1905, after years of negotiations, California transferred the Yosemite Grant back to the federal government to come under the management of Yosemite National Park.

Q. What happened to the size of Yosemite National Park at this time?
1) nothing    2) park got bigger    3) park got smaller
A. 3) Soon after Yosemite National Park was set aside in 1890,

---

*Electricity came to the park in 1902, when the State of California built a powerhouse on one of the Happy Isles.*

business interests began lobbying for legislation to remove from protection almost all of the park's sugar pine forests along the western boundary and transfer them to the Sierra Forest Reserve. Pressure also mounted from mining and grazing interests to reduce park size. All through the 1890s these industries lobbied for boundary changes. In 1905 they succeeded and Congress approved the elimination of 542 square miles from the 1890 park boundary. Lost in this boundary change were not only the sugar pine forests, but also the Minarets, Mt. Ritter, Devil's Postpile, the wintering grounds of park deer and bighorn sheep, and salmon habitat on the lower Merced and Tuolumne rivers. In 1906 more park land was transferred to Sierra Forest Reserve on the west side of the park and the forest in this area was soon logged.

Q. Which President approved this reduction in the size of Yosemite National Park?
1) William H. Taft   2) Theodore Roosevelt   3) Woodrow Wilson

A. 2) Roosevelt had been an ardent supporter of national parks, but he had become a major proponent of forester Gifford Pinchot's philosophy of managing forests for multiple uses such a logging, mining, hunting, grazing as well as recreation and conservation.

*Roosevelt and John Muir*

Q. Did anyone oppose this reduction in the size of Yosemite National Park?
A. Throughout the 1890s, the Sierra Club played an active role in halting actions to diminish the size of the park. In 1904, the boundary commissioners invited comment from club leaders. John Muir, Joseph N. LeConte, and William E. Colby, formed a special committee to examine the Yosemite boundary issue, but their advice was ignored.

Q. Was any new land added to the park in 1905?
A. 113 square miles were added to the northern part of the park. Later, in 1914, a small section of Sierra Forest Reserve, west of Crane Flat, was added to the park.

---

*The site of Yosemite Lodge once held the Indian village Koomine, replaced in 1906 by the cavalry headquarters.*

Q. At this time were Indians still living in Yosemite Valley?
A. In 1897 at least nine separate villages existed. They were located where creeks entered the Merced River, mostly on the north side of the valley. In 1889, fifty-two Indians submitted a petition to Congress asking for the right to manage park lands. By 1910 most families lived in the village of Yawokachi behind the current medical clinic. This village had a ceremonial roundhouse and was inhabited until the early 1930s.

Q. When were cars banned from the park?
1) 1901    2) 1906    3) 1907    4) never
A. 3) When the U.S. Cavalry administered the park, officers believed that automobiles and motorcycles were incompatible with the predominant horse-drawn vehicles. To preclude accidents, acting superintendent H.C. Benson banned autos in 1907. Public pressure to drop the ban mounted until Secretary of the Interior Franklin K. Lane partially lifted it in April 1913—allowing autos to enter Yosemite only via the Coulterville Road.

Q. What other form of transportation brought people to the park that same year?
1) buses    2) railroad    3) motor launch
A. 2) On May 15, 1907 the first train from Merced arrived in El Portal.
    Within five years the Yosemite Lumber Company started logging the sugar pines on the south rim of the Merced Canyon. Logs were transported via an incline to the railroad in El Portal and from there via rail cars to a lumber mill at Merced Falls 53 miles away.

Q. What is the biggest cause of accidental death in Yosemite?
1) rock climbing    2) vehicle accidents    3) horseback riding
A. 2) More than 150 people have died from motor vehicle accidents.

Q. In what year did the National Park Service administration start managing the park?
A. The service was established in August 1916 and W.B. Lewis, Yosemite's first NPS superintendent, served for the next twelve years.

---

*When automobiles first were allowed in Yosemite, they had to yield right of way to horse-drawn vehicles.*

### Hetch Hetchy

**Q.** When was a dam built at the lower end of Hetch Hetchy Valley?

**A.** Construction of the dam was started in 1919 and finished four years later. The total cost was $100 million plus the lives of 67 men and one woman. The project pipes water 160 miles, using gravity alone, to water users in San Francisco and 32 other Bay Area communities.

**Q.** Why was the dam constructed?

**A.** The city of San Francisco wanted a reservoir for its water supply. The same year that Hetch Hetchy became part of Yosemite National Park, the mayor of San Francisco proposed damming the Hetch Hetchy Valley. Thirteen years later Mayor Phelan requested a permit from the United States Department of Interior to create a reservoir in Hetch Hetchy Valley. Secretary of the Interior Ethan Hitchcock refused to issue a permit since Hetch Hetchy was in a national park. The City of San Francisco argued that a reservoir would enhance the valley's beauty. In 1912, after Woodrow Wilson was elected president, he appointed former San Francisco City Attorney Franklin Lane Secretary of the Interior. Lane supported the proposal for a dam.

*Hetch Hetchy Valley before the dam.*

**Q.** How could a city build a dam in a national park?

**A.** Congress had to grant approval. Despite opposition from a large number of citizens and a majority of newspapers, Congress passed the Raker Act in 1913, which allowed the flooding the valley.

---

*The first train service into Yosemite cost $18.50 for a round-trip ticket, including a stagecoach ride from El Portal station into the Yosemite Valley.*

Q. In the 1920s, what was the only road kept open to Yosemite Valley all year round?

A. Rangers used a wooden-V snowplow pulled by horses to keep the road from El Portal clear during winter so that mail could arrive at park headquarters.

Q. When was the first woman ranger hired in Yosemite?

A. Claire Marie Hodges, a teacher, became the first female ranger in the park in 1918, working from May to September that year.

*Clair Hodges*

Q. Who was Enid Michaels?

A. In 1921, Enid became the park's second woman to serve as seasonal naturalist. Park visitors were treated to her walks and talks for the next twenty years. Enid was an avid birdwatcher, along with her husband Charles. Her passion for flowers led to creation of a wildflower garden in Yosemite Valley and preparation of over 1,000 pressed plants for the park museum. During her tenure she wrote 537 articles, the most extensive writing about Yosemite to date by of any author.

Q. When did the annual number of park visitors finally exceed 100,000?
1) 1921   2) 1922   3) 1926

A. 2) In 1922 the number of annual visitors passed 100,000 and by 1928 visitation had risen more than 400,000.

Q. What lodging facilities opened in the Yosemite high country in 1923?

A. Hikers' camps at Merced Lake, Tuolumne Meadows, and Tenaya Lake.

Q. When were the majority of new buildings in the new Yosemite Village completed?
1) 1918   2) 1921   3) 1925

A. 3) By the end of 1925, the new post office, Yosemite Museum, and administration buildings were finished as were the studios of

---

*Today's National Park Service uniforms are based on those of the "doughboys," as U.S. Army soldiers fighting in World War I were nicknamed.*

A.C. Pillsbury, H.B. Best, J.T. Boysen, and D.J. Foley. Yosemite Museum was the first educational center constructed in the national park system.

*Yosemite Museum*

**Q.** What is unique about the design of the museum and the administration building?
**A.** Both were designed to blend with their natural setting. Their rustic architectural style focused on building materials such as rocks, logs, and a shake roof give the look of being built by pioneer crafters.

**Q.** How did the public support building the museum?
**A.** In 1923 the Yosemite Museum Association was formed as the first non-profit cooperating association in the park system. The association collected funds for constructing the museum, including a donation of $75,500 from the Laura Spelman Rockefeller Memorial fund.

**Q.** What special items are in the collection?
**A.** It includes plant specimens, Indian baskets, rare photographs and artwork, and John Muir's notebooks.

**Q.** How many books are in the park research library collection?
1) 2,000    2) 8,000    3) more than 10,000
**A.** 3) The more than 10,000 volumes in the research library cover all aspects of the park and include many rare first editions.

**Q.** What was the first fire engine used in Yosemite?
**A.** A 1925 Graham Dodge truck equipped with tanks, a pump, and hoses.

**Q.** Which luxury hotel was built in the valley in 1927?
**A.** The Ahwahnee Hotel, a prominent example of the new park architecture, was built using rock, massive beams made from tree trunks, and concrete molded to look like wood. Park Service

---

*In 1920, Yosemite was the first national park to offer guided nature walks, a feature that NPS soon added to more parks.*

director Stephen Mather believed that luxurious accommodations of this kind would attract wealthy visitors to the parks and thus garner their support for his new agency.

*Ahwahnee Hotel*

**Q.** How much did a room cost per night at the Ahwahnee in the 1930s?
1) $10   2) $20   3) $35
**A.** 1) Despite the $10 a night room rate, which today seems a pittance, the Ahwahnee was a hotel with high standards. Guests were required to dress appropriately for the dining room: a dress for woman and a suit jacket and tie for men. In the 1930s, during one of his many stays in the park, ex-president Herbert Hoover was questioned by staff whether he was indeed a guest because he was wearing his dirty fishing clothes.

**Q.** What was the room rate at the Ahwahnee in 2010?
1) $250   2) $350   3) over $450
**A.** 3) It cost over $450 for standard rooms and over $1,000 a night for suites.

**Q.** If you visited Yosemite National Park in 1929, which entrance stations wouldn't be in their current locations?
1) Tioga Pass   2) Arch Rock   3) South Entrance
4) Big Oak Flat Entrance
**A.** 3) & 4) The South Entrance and Big Oak Flat entrance are on land that wasn't in the park at that time.

**Q.** When did the South Entrance become included in Yosemite National Park?
1) 1921   2) 1930   3) 1936
**A.** 2) On April 14, 1930, President Herbert Hoover signed a proclamation adding 12,000 acres of forest, with large stands of old-growth sugar pines, to the park. John D. Rockefeller matched federal funds with a gift of $293,000 in order to protect the nearby Merced and Tuolumne Groves of Big Trees. Two years later, in 1932, the Wawona addition comprising 8,765 acres was received. This encompasses the area from the South Entrance to Wawona.

---

*The growth of Yosemite: In 1921, there were 10 full-time and 25 seasonal rangers; in 2009, there were 1,125 seasonal and 741 full-time rangers, office staff, and maintenance workers.*

Q. What land was purchased from the Sugar Pine Lumber Company for $1,495,000 and added to the park in 1939?
A. The 7,200-acre Carl Inn Tract, containing mammoth sugar pines, is adjacent to the Rockefeller purchase and includes the Big Oak Flat entrance and surrounding park land.

Q. During the Great Depression, visitation to the park declined so much that the Yosemite Park and Curry Company saw a loss in income. What was its net profit in 1934?
1) $1,500   2) $16,000   3) $33,000
A. 1) Only $1,500 was earned that year.

Q. How many park service campgrounds were there in Yosemite Valley in the mid-1930s?
A. There were five large campgrounds and together they could accommodate as many as 8,000 people a night. Previous to the construction of park service campgrounds, visitors camped pretty much anywhere they could pitch a tent.

Q. How many campers could stay in the valley in 2010?
1) 1,058   2) 2,748   3) 3,936
A. 2) The 464 campsites in the valley can accommodate 2,748 people. Since the 1930s campground space in Yosemite National Park has been reduced due to damage from floods and efforts to protect sensitive park resources. The maximum capacity for the all park campsites in 2010 was 9,372.

Q. What campground tradition started in the 1930s?
A. According to one version, when a little boy named Elmer got lost, his mother started calling his name over and over. Other campers started calling for him too. Finally little Elmer was found, but the name calling didn't stop. Another version states that a teenage boy named Elmer was late for his birthday party and his teenage friends who shouted for him were chastised by a campground ranger for disturbing other campers. Whatever the true origin was, from that time on, calling for Elmer became a nightly tradition for young campers.

---

*The Yosemite Museum holds more than 4 million items. Relatively few are on exhibit, but all are available to researchers.*

**Q.** Which ranger-naturalist started working in 1931 and continued, mostly in Tuolumne Meadows, until his death in 1994 at age 93?
**A.** Carl W. Sharsmith started a seasonal career in the park soon after attending the Yosemite Field School and served as a seasonal park naturalist in Tuolumne Meadows for more than 60 years. After earning a doctorate in botany at U.C. Berkeley, he taught at San Jose State University where

he also established a herbarium. Each summer he returned to Yosemite. During his early years, Carl led campers on hikes all over the high country, some on hikes more than 20 miles long. Carl captivated campfire audiences with his entertaining and educational tales and, as a world expert in alpine botany, he was sought after by botanists. He married Helen Katherine Myers, who attended the field school and also earned her doctorate in

*Carl W. Sharsmith*

botany. They explored the High Sierra, and shared a small cabin in Tuolumne with their two young children. After Carl and Helen divorced, he returned summer after summer, and mentored younger naturalists, introducing new generations to the high country.

**Q.** Who was the first president to visit the park?
**A.** James Garfield visited the park in 1875 when he was still serving as a congressman, five years before he was elected president. Four years later, ex-president Ulysses S. Grant visited Yosemite Valley. The first sitting president to visit Yosemite was Theodore Roosevelt in May 1903.

**Q.** How many U.S. presidents have visited Yosemite?
1) three  2) five  3) seven  4) ten
**A.** 4) A total of ten presidents have visited the park, but only six were president at the time of their visit.

**Q.** Which president camped with John Muir when he visited Yosemite?

---

*John D. Rockefeller's 1930 contribution to Yosemite was the largest single donation for a public land purchase to that date.*

**A.** In May 1903, Theodore Roosevelt and Muir camped at Glacier Point. With them was ranger Charlie Leidig, who did the cooking.

**Q.** Which president walked all the way down from Glacier Point to the valley because he weighed too much to ride a horse?
1) Woodrow Wilson   2) Grover Cleveland
3) William Howard Taft

*William Howard Taft*

**A.** 3) Taft, who weighed over 300 pounds, visited the park in 1909. Afterward, Taft Point was named in his honor.

**Q.** Which president died in San Francisco one day before he planned to visit Yosemite?
**A.** Warren G. Harding planned to visit the park on July 29 and 30, 1923. Unfortunately he suffered a heart attack in San Francisco the day before he could leave for Yosemite, and died on August 2.

**Q.** Which first lady took a four-day trip into the Yosemite high Country in 1934?
**A.** Eleanor Roosevelt and her secretary were accompanied by chief ranger Townsley and three other rangers to Young Lakes, where they camped. During the trip an unnamed lake below Mt. Conness was named Roosevelt Lake in her honor.

**Q.** This president initiated projects in Yosemite that had a lasting effect on park visitors. Who was he and when did he visit to witness the work being completed?
**A.** President Franklin D. Roosevelt visited Yosemite Valley and the Mariposa Grove of Big Trees on July 15, 1938.

**Q.** How did President Kennedy arrive in Yosemite?
**A.** In 1962, JFK arrived in Yosemite Valley in a military helicopter. That evening an especially large fire was built at Glacier Point to make a spectacular fire fall. A year later, Kennedy set up a commission under the leadership of professor Starker Leopold to study park management. As a result of recommended management changes, artificial attractions, such as the fire fall, were halted.

---

*Today Yosemite has thirteen campgrounds, but in the early days campers could pitch their tents wherever they wanted to.*

Q. What major figures visited Yosemite in 1983?

A. Queen Elizabeth and Prince Phillip stayed at the Ahwahnee Hotel in the top-floor suite. Naturalist Ginger Burley, who had spent time in England, was assigned as their guide. One day they told her that they needed some time without reporters and officials. They simply wished to take a hike and learn about the park's plants, animals, and geology. Their scheduled event at the Mariposa Grove was cancelled, and off they went on a walk in the east end of the valley with ranger Burley, and of course a few Secret Service agents trailing along.

Q. Who was the only First Lady who hiked, rather than rode a horse, into the Yosemite high country to stay at Vogelsang High Sierra Camp?
1) Hillary Clinton    2) Barbara Bush    3) Laura Bush

A. 3) Laura Bush, who was accompanied by several friends and guided by Laurel Boyers, the park's chief wilderness ranger.

Q. What future movie star went out on hikes with Carl Sharsmith in the late 1940s?

A. At age 11, Robert Redford went on a long trek with Carl and other park visitors into the Yosemite high country. When he was older, he worked at Curry Village. Later, in the 1980s, after he had become a movie star, Redford helped produce and narrate *Yosemite: The Fate of Heaven*. This award-winning documentary highlighted the potential environmental damage from the park's three million annual visitors. The film featured a lengthy segment with Carl Sharsmith.

Q. What effect did World War II have on the park?

A. By 1940 park annual visitation had reached 500,000, but after the bombing of Pearl Harbor in December 1941 the number of visitors dropped off dramatically. The Yosemite Park and Curry Company was losing money maintaining the Ahwahnee Hotel so when the U.S. Navy suggested renting it, a deal was made. The lounge was turned into a ward for 350 recovering soldiers. The dining room was used as the mess hall. The California National Guard was stationed in the north part of the park to protect San Francisco's Hetch Hetchy and Lake Eleanor reservoirs, and the

*The U.S. Navy paid $55,000 per year to use the Ahwahnee Hotel as a convalescent hospital during World War II.*

U.S. Army used the park for training maneuvers with as many as 800 soldiers and 60 motorized units at once.

**Q.** What was one of the first feature films that used the park for on location filming?

**A.** *Just Jim*, shot in 1915 by Universal Studios, stars Harry Carey as a burglar who is trying to quit the life of crime and somehow ends up in Yosemite!

**Q.** In 1920 the silent film version of which classic novel has scenes shot in Yosemite Valley?
1) *The Last of the Mohicans*   2) *The Covered Wagon*
3) *The Navigator*

**A.** *1) The Last of the Mohicans* starred Wallace Beery, famed for his later role in *Treasure Island*, and Barbara Bedford, who later played Alfalfa's mother in numerous "Little Rascals" episodes.

**Q.** In 1945, which film starring Van Johnson, playing a soldier, and Esther Williams as a swimming instructor, features scenes in Yosemite?
1) Mountain Mermaid 2) Thrill of a Romance 3) Lake of Dreams

**A.** 2) Thrill of a Romance. With a tagline of "musical bliss with every kiss" and scenes of Williams in her swim suit in Yosemite, how could it go wrong?

**Q.** Which cartoon character, named after the park, first appeared on screen in 1945?

**A.** Yosemite Sam was created by animator Friz Freleng as a new nemesis for Bugs Bunny, taking the place of Elmer Fudd in the cartoon *Hare Trigger*.

**Q.** Who did Yosemite Sam's voice for most of the cartoons?

**A.** Mel Blanc, who also did the voice of Bugs

*Mel Blanc*

---

*Yosemite Sam was based on animator Friz Freleng's own gruff and excitable personality.*

Bunny, Porky Pig, Daffy Duck, Sylvester the Cat, Tweety Bird, Foghorn Leghorn, Wile E. Coyote, Woody Woodpecker, and many other Warner Brothers cartoon characters.

Q. Which acting duo camps in Yosemite in the 1954 comedy *The Long, Long Trailer*?
1) Lucille Ball Lucy and Desi Arnaz
2) Spencer Tracy and Katherine Hepburn
3) Bob Hope and Dorothy Lamour

*Lucille Ball & Desi Arnaz*

A. 1) Rangers posed for photos with celebrities Lucy and Desi when they played the role of madcap campers in Yosemite.

Q. What popular British comedy film, filmed in 1975, used stock footage of Yosemite Valley?
A. *Monty Python and the Holy Grail*.

Q. Which actor had rock climbing instruction in the park before performing in the 1975 film *The Eiger Sanction*?
1) Burt Reynolds    2) Clint Eastwood    3) Steve McQueen
A. Cinematographer Mike Hoover taught Eastwood how to climb over several weeks during the summer of 1974.

Q. What science fiction movie used Yosemite to film scenes in 1988?
1) *Blade Runner*    2) *Aliens*    3) *Star Trek V: The Final Frontier*
A. *Star Trek V*. On vacation in Yosemite, Captain Kirk faces two challenges: climbing El Capitan and teaching campfire songs to Spock. Their vacation is cut short when a renegade Vulcan hijacks the *Enterprise*, and pilots it on a journey to uncover the universe's innermost secrets.

Q. What western was shot on location in Yosemite in 1993?
1) *Shane*    2) *Maverick*    3) *Dances with Wolves*
A. A major scene in *Maverick*, starring Mel Gibson, was shot in the valley in the meadow across from the chapel. The production company donated money to pay for a planned chapel restoration project when they learned about it.

---

*The production crew of* Star Trek V *got into trouble with the park service for painting a cliff to get better lighting while filming a climbing scene.*

**Q.** In what classic novel by Jack Kerouac do two crazed beatniks ascend Yosemite's Matterhorn peak?
1) *On the Road*   2) *Dharma Bums*   3) *Howl*
**A.** 2) *Dharma Bums* is based on a climb of Matterhorn by Kerouac, Gary Snyder and John Montgomery in 1955.

*Jack Kerouac*

**Q.** Which mystery novels take place in Yosemite?
1) *The Affair of the Jade Monkey*
2) *A Body To Dye For*   3) *High Country*
**A.** All of the above.

**Q.** In which science fiction novel do the Royal Arches collapse and Half Dome crumble?
**A.** *The Forge of God*, by Greg Bear

**Q.** Which TV series took place in Yosemite in the 1970s?
**A.** In the fall of 1974, NBC shot *Sierra* on location in Yosemite and was advised by Yosemite Park rangers. The series starred Jack Hogan as Chief Ranger Jack Moore, Mike Warren as Ranger P.J. Lewis, and Susan Foster as Ranger Julie Beck. Episodes were about rangers protecting campers from bears, rescuing lost campers and enforcing regulations. A frequent character on the show was the troublesome bear named Cruncher.

**Q.** How long did it run?
**A.** 3 months.

**Q.** Who wrote the theme song?
1) Johnny Cash   2) Stevie Wonder   3) John Denver
**A.** 3) Singer/songwriter John Denver, as well as creating the theme song, actually appeared in one episode.

**Q.** Which African American television personality camped in Yosemite in October 2010?
**A.** Oprah Winfrey and her traveling companion, Gayle King, camped in a pop-up trailer in Yosemite Valley and met with

---

*All that remains of Wah-ho-ga village are medicinal plants that the Indian residents planted around their cabins.*

Yosemite's lone full-time black ranger, Shelton Johnson. Johnson wrote the novel *Gloryland*, based on the history of the "buffalo soldiers." Oprah visited the park after receiving a letter from him remarking on the small number of African American visitors. Johnson took her on a tour, and later attended her show.

*Johnson in "buffalo soldier" uniform*

**Q.** What percentage of Yosemite's visitors are African-American?
**A.** A 2009 Park Service study estimated that, of the approximately 3.87 million visitors to Yosemite that year, 1% were "African American or black." That same year it was estimated that blacks made up 13.5% of the total U.S. population. Another 11% were "Asian and Latinos," with the remainder being "white."

**Q.** Which San Francisco cartoonist created a cartoon strip that featured bears, campers, and rangers in Yosemite?
1) Matt Groening   2) Al Capp   3) Phil Frank
**A.** Phil Frank's comic strip *Farley* first appeared in the *San Francisco Chronicle* in 1975, and characters such as Alphonse the bear and Velma Melmac entertained readers for the next 32 years.

**Q.** What was Mission 66 and what effect did it have on the park?
**A.** In 1956, Park Service Director Conrad Wirth introduced the Mission 66 program, a 10-year, billion-dollar program to restore and update park facilities before the National Park Service's 50th anniversary. In Yosemite this resulted in the Yosemite Valley Visitor Center, park service housing and a new elementary school in El Portal, and a variety of road projects. The most controversial project was paving the Tioga Road, which was protested by the Sierra Club. Ansel Adams, a club member, as well as NPS Naturalist Carl Sharsmith, voiced their opposition to this project.

**Q.** Which ski cabin was "re-discovered" in the 1960s?
**A.** The Snow Creek Cabin, used by skiers before the opening of Badger Pass, had been long forgotten. Hidden in a thick grove of

---

*Mission 66 improved access to Yosemite, which in turn helped lead to overcrowding in the 1960s.*

fir trees, it hadn't been used for years. A young park employee out hiking found it, and told some of her friends. Before long, young people started living in the cabin. They planted a garden that included both vegetables and marijuana plants. It was quite a while before the rangers found out. At this time, cross-country skiing was becoming popular in Yosemite. A chief ranger supportive of backcountry skiing allowed one of the hut's young residents to volunteer as its winter keeper, but the cabin was closed to summer residents. Around the same time, Ostrander Ski Hut, which had been closed for some years, was re-opened and staffed with a ranger for the winter. Both cabins are now open for winter use.

Q. What happened to the Indian villages in Yosemite Valley?
A. In the 1930s the park administration had begun searching for a location for a "new" Indian village. A site east of Rocky Point below Eagle Peak was decided on. This village, Wah-ho-ga, consisted of fifteen cabins housing most of the Indian families. Some of the cabins later were razed or relocated by the government and by the late 1950s only six cabins remained. By 1960 three cabins stood in Wah-ho-ga, and the last house was torn down in 1969. As of 2010 one of the relocated cabins stood in the maintenance area north of the museum building.

Q. Which park feature has become an icon for Yosemite?
A. Half Dome. Starting in 1968, the Yosemite Park and Curry Company began using a stylized logo of the dome. Despite the changes in the companies running the park concession, the logo

continues to be used. It appears on everything from hoodies to jewelry, golf bags, and tongue rings.

Q. What countercultural confrontation occurred in Yosemite on July 4, 1970?
A. A riot occurred when young people camping and partying in Stoneman Meadow refused to leave. Rangers reacted in a heavy-handed way, giving a deadline for departure without attempting to inform the campers about the damage they were causing to the

---

*When Ostrander Ski Hut was completed inn 1940, it was the park's final Civilian Conservation Corps project. Workers used rock and logs from the site to build the two-story alpine-style lodge.*

meadow. When rangers posted closure signs, these were torn down and thrown into the river. In response, rangers led a horseback charge into the meadow. Dr. John Fisher, a former Republican state senator from Florida, who was in the valley with his family, wrote to President Nixon asking what he should tell his children about the rangers' brutality that he and his family witnessed. Eventually, new and younger seasonal rangers were hired, who knew how to communicate with the '60s generation.

Q. When was the Yosemite General Management Plan or GMP started?
A. The initial work for the plan was started in the early 1970s and culminated with three volumes published August 1978, January 1980, and September 1980. The stated goals were to reclaim priceless natural beauty, markedly reduce traffic congestion, allow natural processes to prevail, reduce crowding, and promote visitor understanding and enjoyment.

Q. Were the above goals achieved?
A. After the plan was released and before it could be enacted, park visitation rose to 3 million visitors, and then reached 4 million visitors before dropping for a decade, and then climbed that high again in 2009. With this increase came increased traffic congestion and crowding. Strides were made in fire management and habitat restoration, but there remain conflicts between development and allowing natural processes to occur. One example is new armoring being added to river banks after the flood of 1997.

Q. Has the plan been enacted?
A. Due to lawsuits by organizations challenging the legality of separate Yosemite plans, the GMP has not been implemented. In October 2009, the U.S. Court of Appeals for the Ninth Circuit determined that the NPS Merced River Plan failed to set a "maximum quantity of use" for the river area and too narrowly defined the boundaries for the El Portal section of the wild and scenic river. Without the river plan's being approved, other plans in the Merced River corridor, which includes Yosemite Valley and El Portal, cannot be enacted.

---

*Yosemite National Park has sister parks—Torres del Paine in Chile and Huangshun (Yellow Mountain) and Jiuzhaigou national parks in China. They work together to protect these magnificent areas.*

**Q.** When did Yosemite have its first female superintendent?

**A.** Barbara J. Griffin was appointed to Yosemite's top park service post in 1995. During her tenure, in 1996, annual visitation exceeded 4 million, but then dropped the following year due to the flood of 1997. Visitation did not reach that level again until 2009. In the early 1970s there were very few women working for the park service in Yosemite, and none in administrative positions. By the new millennium there were many women branch chiefs, but as of 2010 there has yet to be a woman chief ranger or head of maintenance.

**Q.** What has been named after El Capitan?
1) a hotel   2) a theater   3) a coffee company

**A.** All of the above.

**Q.** What kinds of things have Yosemite in their name?
1) wine label    2) fruit brand
3) office building

**A.** The Yosemite Building in Los Angles was the first home of the Los Angeles Oil Exchange. Yosemite Road Wine has a Modesto appellation. Several fruit companies from the early 1900s had a Yosemite

brand. Their crate labels featured pictures of giant sequoias, the view from Inspiration Point, and other Yosemite locales.

---

*The first year that park visitation exceeded
3 million people was 1987.*

## QUOTE QUEST #6

*Find the underlined words in eight different directions from this quote by Lafayette Bunnell about evicting the Ahwahneechee from Yosemite Valley in 1851:* "It was **therefore decided** that the best **policy** was to **destroy** their **huts** and **stores**, with a view of **starving** them out, and thus **compelling** them to come in and **join** with Ten-ie-ya and the **people** with him on the **reservation**." *When all the underlined words have been crossed out, the remaining letters will spell what Tenaya said.*

```
R D L E N T U S R E M A I
E N E I N I T H E E C M O
S U N S T A O I N R O E S
E W H E T R E J W O M L E
R W E R E R B O R F P P N
V ; W H E R O E T E E O H
A E H A S H E Y D R L E S
T O U F O U S E R E L P F
I A T T H T D E R H I S H
O A S V O I E B E T N E N
N G I R C V E N T O G T H
E W E E I G N I V R A T S
N S D D P O L I C Y S Q C
```

Hidden message: "___ __ _____ __ ___

_____ ____ __ ____ ____ ____

___ _____ __ ___ _____ ____ ____

____ __ ___ ____"

---

*Tour buses and non-summer visitors have helped increase park visitation, along with regional population growth.*

## Quote Quest #7

*Find the underlined words in eight different directions from this quote by Ansel Adams describing Yosemite Valley:* "**Yosemite Valley**, to me, is **always** a **sunrise**, a **glitter** of **green** and **golden wonder** in a **vast** **edifice** of **stone** and **space**." *When all the underlined words have been crossed out, the remaining letters will spell what ranger-naturalist Carl Sharsmith said to a park visitor who asked him what he would do if he only had an hour to spend in the park.*

```
N E D L O G Y E I W
O U L D G E O T S G
I S T I L N E I E L
R T U L H N E M D I
S E A N O M G E I T
P V D T R R E S F T
A T S N E I A O I E
C S D E O O S Y C R
E A N W A W N E E D
C V A L W A Y S R Y
```

Hidden message: "_  _ _ _ _ _   _ _   _ _ _   _ _   _ _ _

_ _ _ _ _ _   _ _ _   _ _ _"

---

*Prospectors explored for gold near Mono Pass, Upper Gaylor Lake, and Mt. Hoffman—but, luckily for future Yosemite National Park, none of these produced a mine.*

# RECREATION

Q. How many miles of hiking trails are in Yosemite?
1) more than 200   2) more than 600   3) more than 800
A. 3) There are over 800 miles of official trails in the park, and dozens of miles of "use trails" that have been created by climbers, fishing enthusiasts, and other hikers.

Q. Is walking off-trail legal in the park?
A. Heavily visited zones may be cordoned off to allow for restoration of natural conditions, but in most areas of the park it is legal to walk anywhere. Of course, wet meadows, lakeshores and other wetland areas can be damaged by footsteps, so hikers are encouraged to choose walking routes that avoid these delicate communities. Off-trail hikers should know how to orient themselves using topographic maps to prevent becoming lost. The creation of new or "shortcut" trails is seriously discouraged.

Q. Which long-distance trails go through the park?
1) the John Muir Trail   2) the High Sierra Trail   3) the Pacific Crest Trail
A. 1) & 3) The 211-mile John Muir Trail stretches from Happy Isles

in Yosemite Valley to Mt. Whitney. Its lowest point is 4,035' and the highest is 14,496' at the summit of Mt. Whitney. Starting in Canada, 2,650-mile Pacific Crest Trail continues through mountains all the way to Mexico. It follows the John Muir Trail for 160 miles and then continues south via a different route.

Q. What other two national parks do both trails traverse?
A. Sequoia and Kings Canyon.

Q. How many miles long is the roundtrip hike to the top of Half Dome?
1) 15   2) 17   3) 20
A. 2) The elevation gain on the 17-mile roundtrip hike to Half Dome is about 4,900'. The final 200 yards requires using cables fixed on posts to ascend to the summit. Over the years, more than 20 people have died on the dome. It is extremely hazardous during thunderstorms, due to the chance of lightning hits and the increased danger of slipping on the smooth rock.

Q. How many people were estimated to have hiked to the top of the dome in 2008?
1) 21,000   2) 58,000   3) 84,000
A. 3) 84,000! In 2009, two people died from falling while ascending the cables. The park service realized that the extreme crowding was making the final part of the hike more dangerous, especially on weekends when an average of 840 people were going up the cables in one day.

Q. How many people have been killed by lightning while on Half Dome?
1) 1   2) 3   3) 12
A. 2) A total of three people have been killed on the dome during thunderstorms. Two of them were part of group of young men who ascended as storm was building and continued despite warnings by descending hikers that it would be too dangerous to proceed.

---

*Lightning storms are more dangerous to Half Dome climbers than is the threat of falling.*

Q. When were limits placed on the number of hikers per day who could go up Half Dome?
A. In May 2010, the national park service started a pilot program requiring permits to hike up Half Dome on Fridays through Sundays and on holidays. On these days only 400 were issued per day.

Q. Which waterfall is the most visited in Yosemite Valley?
1) Lower Yosemite Falls   2) Bridalveil Fall   3) Ribbon Fall
A. The trail to the bridge at the base of Lower Yosemite Falls is a mere one-quarter mile from the road and very close to bus parking at Yosemite Lodge, and thus gets the largest number of visitors.

Q. Which waterfall attracts the largest number of hikers to its top?
1) Yosemite Falls   2) Snow Creek Falls   3) Vernal Fall
A. The hike to the lip of Vernal Fall is only 1.5 miles via the popular Mist Trail, and thus a large number of visitors are able to reach it.

Q. From 1913 to 2005 how many people died in the park after falling over a waterfall?
A. Forty-two.

Q. Which waterfall accounted for the most deaths?
Eleven people have died at Vernal Fall. More hikers make it to the top of Vernal Fall than any other major Yosemite waterfall.
A. Unfortunately, too many of them think it's safe to swim or wade in the river above the falls. During high water, some are swept over the lip by the powerful current.

Q. Are park streams and rivers safe to swim in?
A. Every year, in the late spring and early summer, park visitors drown when trying to swim in cold, fast-flowing water. Over 150 people have drowned in Yosemite waters. Swimming is safer in mid- to late summer when water temperatures are warmer and flows are diminished.

Q. Is it legal to raft in the Yosemite Valley?
A. Rafts can be used on the Merced River between Stoneman (near

---

*Late spring and early summer are unsafe times to swim in Yosemite's streams: the water is too cold and fast-flowing!*

Curry Village) and Sentinel Beach Picnic Area between the hours of 10 A.M. and 6 P.M. when the river depth at Sentinel Bridge is less than 6.5', and the sum of air and water temperatures is more than 100° F. Personal flotation devices are required. Rafts can be rented at Curry Village. Private canoes, kayaks, and rafts may be used on this section of the Merced, but no other parts of the river.

Q. What other locations in the park are legal to raft or boat in?
A. Non-motorized boating is also permitted on the South Fork of Merced in Wawona, Tenaya Lake, and Lake Eleanor, but not on Hetch Hetchy Reservoir.

Q. Is there whitewater rafting or kayaking near the park?
A. Yes. Sections of the Merced and Tuolumne rivers are suitable for various levels of whitewater sports. Numerous commercial rafting companies provide one- or two-day trips in season.

Q. It's safe to drink out of any of the park's streams, rivers, or lake—true or false?
A. False. In past times, when there were fewer park visitors, it was possible to drink from lakes and streams, but beginning in the late 1960s hikers started getting sick from ingesting giardia, a minute protozoan, that was becoming more common in fresh water. It takes a while for people who get sick from drinking water

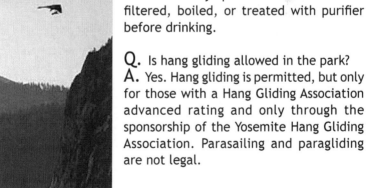

infected with giardia to realize it because the illness takes one to two weeks before victims feel symptoms. Water should be filtered, boiled, or treated with purifier before drinking.

Q. Is hang gliding allowed in the park?
A. Yes. Hang gliding is permitted, but only for those with a Hang Gliding Association advanced rating and only through the sponsorship of the Yosemite Hang Gliding Association. Parasailing and paragliding are not legal.

---

*Because of intensive park visitation, Yosemite's lake and stream waters must be treated before drinking.*

Q. Who died in 1998 while attempting a record free fall jump in the park?
A. Dan Osman was well known for his daredevil rope jumps off high cliffs. On November 23, 1998, Osman leapt off a rock pillar called Leaning Tower and fell 1,100'. On this attempt to break his previous record, the strain on the rope was too great. When it broke, Osman plummeted to his death.

Q. Is BASE jumping legal in Yosemite?
A. No. At first the park service tried to regulate BASE jumping for safety and resource reasons. They agreed to make it legal if jumpers agreed to restrictions of limited jump sites and times and asked for help from the U.S. Parachute Association. BASE jumpers threatened to sue the association and demanded that they be free of regulations. This led to a total banning of the sport.

Q. What happened in October 1999 during a jump to protest this ban?
A. A group of five BASE jumpers asked media to attend an illegal jump from El Capitan to protest the death of another jumper in June of that year. That jumper had died trying to escape from rangers waiting to arrest him after he landed in El Capitan Meadow. To avoid capture he jumped into the river, which was at a high flow level, and drowned. During the protest jump, one of the five jumpers plunged to her death when her chute failed to open.

Q. Who started the Yosemite Winter Club?
1) Sierra Club    2) National Park Service   3) Curry Company
A. 3) The purpose of this club, created by the Curry Company, was to promote competitions in various winter sports and to lobby for improvement of winter facilities. It offered multiple snow-based events, including ski-joring, where horses pulled skiers on a track in Stoneman Meadow.

---

*In 1928, the Yosemite Winter Club sponsored weekly ski-jumping competitions, intercollegiate hockey, figure skating, costume-skating events, curling, and tobogganing.*

Q. Who was the first president of the winter club?
1) Ansel Adams    2) Horace Albright    3) Mary Curry Tressider
A. 2) Horace Albright, who had been assistant director under Park Service Director Stephen Mather, served briefly as Yosemite Park Superintendent and then as Director of NPS.

Q. When was the Yosemite Ski School started?
1) 1923    2) 1926    3) 1928

A. 3) Headed by Jules Fritsch, the school opened in 1928, and was the first of its kind in the West.

Q. Which Yosemite residents were founding members of the California Ski Association in 1930?
A. Donald Tressider and Ernst DesBaillets, the Curry Company winter sports director, were among the 16 original members. This new organization cosponsored the Winter Sports Carnival in Yosemite in the winter of 1929-30.

Q. What was the highlight of the carnival that year?
A. Skiers were towed behind ranger Frank Gallison's airplane (its wings removed). Other special events were ashcan sliding, baseball on snowshoes, and a Mardi Gras on ice. Even dogsled rides were provided. The event attracted 3,700 people, as both audience and participants.

Q. What transportation option did the Curry Company investigate to move visitors to deeper snow on the valley rim at Glacier Point or Snow Creek?
A. Consultants were hired in 1930 to research the possibility of using cable tramways like the ones operated in the Alps. Though cable tramways have been proposed several times in the park's history, they have never been built.

Q. What major event did the Yosemite Winter Club try to bring to the park in 1932?
A. Despite lobbying help from the California State Government

---

*In 2009, 75% of Yosemite visitors were from the U.S., and most of the other 25% were from European nations.*

and the National Park Service to bring the international Winter Olympics to Yosemite, the event ended up taking place in Lake Placid, New York.

Q. Between 1930 and 1935, the Curry Company, under the leadership of Donald and Mary Curry Tressider, offered three different guided cross-country ski tours to huts in the park. Where did the trips go?
A. These overnight trips went to Snow Creek Cabin, Glacier Point Mountain House, and from Yosemite Valley to Tuolumne Meadows. During the six-day journey to Tuolumne, the groups—provided with guide and cook—stayed at ranger stations at Tenaya Lake, Tuolumne and Merced Lake. Food was stashed at these stations in late fall.

*Donald and Mary Curry Tressider*

Q. Where did Curry envision building new huts?
A. Since the company had the use of the Glacier Point Mountain House in the winter, a location between Ostrander Lake and Merced Lake appeared to make sense. The idea of a high camp at Royal Arch Lake was also discussed.

Q. When did downhill skiing operations begin in the Glacier Point Road area?
A. After the Wawona Tunnel opened in June 1933, downhill skiing took place at Chinquapin after the next three winters. The Curry Company operated a shuttle to Monroe Meadows (Badger Pass) so skiers could have a long run back down to the Wawona Road.

Q. When did Badger Pass Ski lodge open?
A. The ski lodge was built in Monroe Meadow in 1935, and in 1936 the first ski lift in the West, called the Upski, was installed. This was a large sled that was pulled up and down the slope on a cable. Nicknamed the "Queen Mary," it could carry six skiers at a time. As of 2010 it was still operating under the management of the park concessions.

---

*Monroe Meadows was named for George Monroe,*
*an African-American stage coach driver and guide who*
*worked for the Yosemite Stage Company from 1868 to 1886.*

Q. Nic Fiore, who was ski instructor and head of the ski school, worked at Badger Pass for 57 years. How many people is it estimated that he taught?
1) 65,000   2) 93,000   3) 137,000
A. 3) During his long career Nic taught at least 137,000 people to ski, many of them from different generations in the same families.

Q. Skating is another winter sport with a history in Yosemite Valley. Winters in the early years of the park were colder than at present, which meant there was sufficient ice at Mirror Lake, and portions of the Merced River on "natural" skating rinks. When was an artificial rink built in the Valley?
A. In 1928, the Yosemite Winter Club flooded a parking lot at Curry Village. Later a permanent rink was built, equipped with warming hut and fire pit.

Q. Why is there a golf course in Yosemite?
A. A dilemma that faced the national park system was insuring there would be enough supporters of the parks to prevent them from being transferred to the U.S. Forest Service or private hands. Luxury hotels and opportunities to play sports like tennis and golf made the park experience more appealing for wealthy urbanites.

Since the 1970s the park service has been re-examining many of these sports facilities in an effort to balance, first, the public's desire to entertain themselves with some sports that may not be appropriate in parks and, second, with the Park Service's goal of protecting wildlife. For example, Wawona Meadow, where the golf course was built, is nesting habitat for the rare great gray owl and the endangered willow flycatcher.

---

*The public is not as interested in national parks with golf courses as it once was, and the National Park Service avoids adding new ones.*

Q. For many summers, what activity did many of the younger Yosemite Valley visitors look forward to?

A. Beginning in 1922, with the construction of a dance pavilion at Camp Curry, young folks pursued romantic encounters on the dance floor. After a long hike, and hopefully a bath, shower or swim, a dance was special conclusion to a day in the mountains. Curry Village also boasted a pool hall, a soda fountain, and a swimming pool with lifeguard. Only the pool remains today.

Q. What question do park rangers hear most?
A. Where's the bathroom?

*When Camp Curry was established in 1899, its goal was to offer families lodging for less than the $4.00 per night.*

# CLIMBING HISTORY

**Q.** Who first scaled Mt. Conness and Mt. Clark?
**A.** In 1866 Clarence King and James T. Gardner of Whitney Geological Survey were the first climbers to summit these peaks.

**Q.** Most mountaineers who scale Cathedral Peak in Tuolumne Meadows are roped up for the last thirty feet. Who made the first recorded ascent in 1869—without any climbing gear?
**A.** John Muir.

**Q.** When was the first ascent of Mt. Lyell accomplished?
**A.** In 1871, John Bois Tileston of Boston reached the top.

**Q.** In Josiah Whitney's 1869 edition of his *Yosemite Guide-Book* he wrote that Half Dome was "probably the only one of all the prominent points about the Yosemite which never has been, and never will be, trodden by human foot." How many years later was he proven wrong?
1) three    2) six    3) fifteen
**A.** 2) Six years later, on October 12, 1875, George Anderson reached the top of Half Dome. Anderson, a blacksmith in Yosemite

Valley, drilled holes and inserted eye bolts one by one, about five to six feet apart. He tied his rope to each bolt as it was placed and then stood on the highest bolt and used a hand drill and single jack to make a hole for the next bolt. He continued placing bolt after bolt until he reached the top in less than a week's time. Galen Clark, at age sixty-one, and Sally Dutcher, assistant to photographer Carleton Watkins, became some of the first people to take Anderson's route to top of the dome. Later, Anderson guided several groups of tourists up his route, so in addition to placing the route he was probably the first of a long line of Yosemite Valley climbing guides.

The current trail reaches the back side of Half Dome via a set of steep switchbacks up Sub-dome to cables placed by the Sierra Club in 1919 near Anderson's old route.

Q. Who took the first photograph from the top of Half Dome?
A. James Hutchings, guided by Anderson, took along his 13-year-old daughter Florence, his 65-year-old mother-in-law, and photographer S.D. Walker. Walker captured the first photographic images from the summit.

Q. When was the cable placed on the backside of Half Dome?
A. In 1919, the Sierra Club installed the metal posts and steel cables.

Q. What major first ascents in Yosemite Valley were accomplished by Bestor Robinson and Dick Leonard in 1934?
A. Lower and Upper Cathedral Spires, which had long been eyed by climbers as a special challenge.

*Cathedral Spires*

Q. What change in climbing gear contributed to climbers of the late 1940s accomplishing more difficult climbs in Yosemite Valley?
A. Sierra Club climbers who had joined the 10th Mountain Division during WWII brought back new

---

*Enid Michael, one of the earliest women naturalist-rangers here, also was one of the first women climbers—with her husband Charles.*

equipment such as wafer-thin pitons, aluminum carabiners and nylon ropes. Perhaps the most useful of this new gear was the nylon rope that was much better than the old hemp ropes because the lead climber could take a longer fall without the rope's breaking. Nylon is elastic and stretches, easing the fall.

Q. Which pioneering Yosemite climber forged hard steel pitons out of Model A Ford axles?
A. Swiss-born John Salathé, a blacksmith, changed Yosemite climbing with the creation of these harder pitons that could be used over and over in solid Yosemite rock.

Q. What climb did Salathé accomplish first in 1946?
A. Climbing with Ax Nelson, he made the first ascent up the face of Half Dome. During the twenty-hour climb they slept on a ledge before summiting the following morning. This was probably the first bivouac on a Yosemite climb. At age forty-six, Salathé became a pioneer in Yosemite big-wall climbing with this major accomplishment.

Q. What pair of climbers first scaled the northwest face of Half Dome?
A. Royal Robbins and Jerry Gallwas in 1955.

Q. How many days did it take to make the first ascent of the Nose route on El Capitan?
A. On November 12, 1958 after twelve days of climbing, Warren Harding, George Whitmore, and Wayne Merry reached the summit. Less than two years later, in September 1960, Royal Robbins, Chuck Pratt, Joe Fitschen, and Tom Frost become the second party to ascend the Nose. They climbed it without using fixed ropes in almost half the time as Harding and party.

*During the 1960s and '70s, climbers gave routes intriguing names such as Bongs Away, Mescalito, and Tangerine Trip.*

Q. Who accomplished the first solo climb of a Yosemite big wall?
A. In May of 1963, Royal Robbins, during four days of storms, made a solo ascent of the west face of Leaning Tower.

Q. Who were the first women climbers to make an ascent of El Capitan?
A. In 1973, Sibylle Hechtel and Bev Johnson used the Triple Direct route to reach the summit of El Capitan. Five years later Bev Johnson made the first female solo ascent of El Capitan by climbing the Dihedral Wall.

Q. During the 1970s, there was a culture clash between law enforcement rangers and climbers. What did they do to find common ground?
A. Baseball games, climbers versus rangers, were played at the Yosemite Valley elementary school baseball diamond. Though the climbers' teams boasted some of the best athletes on the planet, such as John Bachar and Ron Kauk, the rangers were usually the baseball champs.

Q. What accident led to dozens of climbers trekking on snowshoes and skis to Lower Merced Pass Lake in the winter of 1976-77?
A. A twin-engine Lodestar with a full cargo of marijuana crash-landed into the icy lake in December 1976. Rangers believed it would be safe from salvagers, but word of the cargo got out and young mountaineers, many of them rock climbers, traveled through the backcountry to this remote lake. Despite the dead pilot and crew in the plane, marijuana was salvaged from the fuselage. Some scavengers even brought in scuba gear to recover the costly cargo carried from Mexico. By the time rangers discovered that the cargo was being salvaged, much of it had been hauled out and sold.

Q. Who completed the first solo ascent of El Capitan in one day?
A. In 1987 Jim Beyer made this record climbing a route up West Face of El Capitan.

Q. What climbing event in 1989 attracted major media coverage?
A. Paraplegic Mark Wellman and partner Mike Corbett climbed

---

*On a stained glass window in the synagogue of the Sherith Israel Congregation, San Francisco, Moses with the tablets containing the Ten Commandments is shown descending from El Capitan.*

the shield on El Capitan. Using specially designed equipment, Wellman ascended the entire way without the use of his legs. Later, in 1991, Wellman and Corbett climbed the face of Half Dome. It took thirteen days and like the previous accomplishment, became international news. Mike Corbett had previously climbed El Capitan more than forty times.

Q. What major climbing first was accomplished in 1993?
A. Lynn Hill climbed the Nose route of El Capitan with Brooke Sandahl, free climbing every pitch to make the first free ascent of this famous big wall. A year later Lynn Hill, on the same route but belayed by Steve Sutton, reached the top in less than twenty-four hours.

Q. As of 2010, what was the fastest climb of the nose route on El Capitan?
A. In July 2008 Hans Florine and Yuji Hirayama reached the tree that serves as the finish line in a mere 2 hours, 43 minutes and 33 seconds. On November 6, 2010, climbers Dean Potter and Sean Leary set a new speed record via the Nose route on El Capitan in Yosemite National Park, scaling the giant granite monolith in 2 hours, 36 minutes, 45 seconds.

Q. Between 1906 and 2006, how many hikers died from hiking or scrambling over rock?
A. Over 120, of which 20 were park residents.

Q. What is the annual estimate of number of climber user days is the park? (A user day is one climber for one day.)
1)10- to 15,000    2) 25- to 50,000   3) 60- to 70,000.
A. 2) 25- to 50,000.

Q. The Yosemite search and rescue team had the greatest number of search and rescue incidents in 1990. How many were there?
A. 300.

*More than 22 climbers have died on El Capitan, and 60 more climbing fatalities have occurred on other big-wall climbs.*

## *Puzzlers*

### YOSEMITE BY NUMBERS

All answers are numeric and are be found throughout the text.

*Across*
1. The number of bird species sighted in the park exceeds...
2. Humans have occupied Yosemite for at least this many years...
3. How many species of native rodents call Yosemite home?
5. How many trees were toppled by the windblast from the Happy Isles rockslide?
6. The number of miles of official trails in the park is greater than...
7. How many acres of park were allowed to burn from naturally caused fires in 2007?
8. This many domestic sheep were removed from the park by Yosemite's first rangers in 1898.
9. In 1987 total park visitation reached this number for the first time.
10. How many cabins were removed after the rockslide at Curry Village in 1999?
11. It has been this number of years since a glacier was in Yosemite Valley.
12. The John Muir Trail is this many miles long.
13. There are this many butterfly species in the park.
14. A peregrine falcon can fly this many miles per hour.
15. The heaviest known park bear weighed in at this number of pounds.

*Down*
1. How many calories does a black bear consume on an autumn day?
2. The number of items in the Yosemite Museum collection is more than...
4. Between 1877 and 1991 this many fish were stocked in the park's stream, rivers and lakes.
6. This many hikers walked to the top of Half Dome in 2008.
7. How many seeds can a mature giant sequoia tree produce in a single year?
8. The number of conifer species in the park is...

*On average, Yosemite search-and-rescue teams assist 25 climbing groups per year.*

10. This is the height of Yosemite Falls, measured in feet.
11. The park encompasses this many square miles.
14. This is the number of park waterfalls higher than 1,000 feet.

*In October 2004, two Japanese climbers ascending El Capitan were caught in a severe multi-day storm and died of hypothermia after a failed attempt to descend.*

## QUOTE QUEST #8

*Find and cross out the underlined words from this quote by Enid Michael, park naturalist and one of Yosemite's first woman climbers:* "<u>After many climbs</u> of exploration to the <u>base</u> of <u>Half Dome</u> we have come to <u>believe</u> that this <u>chute</u> that <u>throws dust</u> in the <u>face</u> is the only <u>possible route</u> to the first of the <u>great ledges</u>." *When all the underlined words have been crossed out, the remaining letters will spell what Swiss-born climber John Salathé said about climbing regulations in Yosemite.*

| | | | | | | | | |
|---|---|---|---|---|---|---|---|---|
| W | H | E | L | B | I | S | S | O | P |
| Y | C | A | T | H | R | O | W | S | R |
| T | E | V | E | I | L | E | B | N | E |
| T | S | C | L | I | M | B | S | D | T |
| E | L | U | W | B | E | J | O | T | F |
| C | E | R | D | H | A | M | U | A | A |
| A | D | O | S | A | E | S | Y | E | T |
| F | G | U | C | L | L | N | E | R | I |
| M | E | T | B | F | A | L | D | G | J |
| R | S | E | Q | M | C | H | U | T | E |

*Hidden message:* "_ _ _   _ _ _'_   _ _   _ _ _ _   _ _ _ _ _?"

## JOKE

Q. What do you call a hiker with a rash from poison oak?
A. An itch hiker

*El Capitan*

---

*Climbing nearly straight up on El Capitan and Half Dome is appropriately called "big-wall" climbing.*

# PUZZLERS ANSWERS

## YOSEMITE ELEVATION MATCH

| | | |
|---|---|---|
| 1. | Yosemite Valley | 4,000 |
| 2. | Glacier Point | 7,124 |
| 3. | Half Dome | 8,842 |
| 4. | Mt. Lyell | 13,114 |
| 5. | Tuolumne Meadows | 8,600 |
| 6. | Tioga Pass | 9,941 |
| 7. | Wawona | 4,000 |
| 8. | Mariposa Grove | 5,600 |
| 9. | Mt. Hoffman | 10,845 |
| 10. | El Portal | 2,100 |

## QUOTE QUEST #1

"Great is granite and Yosemite is its prophet."—Thomas Starr King

## QUOTE QUEST #2

"The stream entirely dissolves into spray."—William Brewer

137

## FALLS MATCH

1. Yosemite Falls        7
2. Sentinel Falls        4
3. Illilouette Fall      5
4. Vernal Fall           8
5. Nevada Fall           6
6. Ribbon Fall          10
7. Royal Arch Cascade    2
8. Staircase Falls       3
9. Bridalveil Fall       1
10. Horsetail Fall       9

## GEOGRAPHY & GEOLOGY CROSSWORD

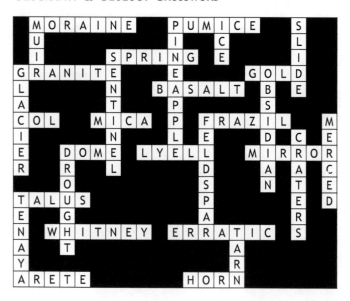

---

*John Muir once scrambled up a 100' Douglas-fir to experience a heavy windstorm by swaying in its branches.*

## QUOTE QUEST #3

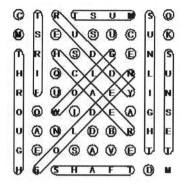

"Come suck sequoia and be saved."—John Muir

## TREE ACROSTIC

Yellow
Oregon
Sequoia
Elm
Mariposa
Incense
Tamarack
Evergreen

## QUOTE QUEST #4

"They warn you not to feed the bears, but they have a hospital for those that do."—Will Rogers

---

*Galen Clark had no use for shoes, and hiked around Yosemite barefoot rather than wear what he called "silly instruments of torture."*

## Yosemite Word Scramble

*Wildlife*
1. great gray owl
2. pika
3. Yosemite toad
4. spotted bat
5. mule deer
6. ringtail cat
7. Pacific fisher
8. black swift
9. mountain kingsnake
10. black bear
11. Steller's jay

*Things*
12. sequoia
13. waterfall
14. cliff
15. orchid
16. glacier
17. whitebark pine
18. rockslide
19. lightning

*Places*
20. Tuoulumne
21. Glacier Point
22. El Capitan

## Quote Quest #5

"Swifter than swift is the white-throated swift."—William Leon Dawson, *Birds of California* (1923)

---

## Quote Quest #6

"Let us remain in the mountains where we were born; where the ashes of our fathers have been given to the winds."—Tenaya, 1851

## Quote Quest #7

"I would go sit by the meadow and cry."—Carl Sharsmith

*The buildings comprising Pioneer Yosemite History Center at Wawona were moved there in the 1950s and 1960s from all over the park.*

## YOSEMITE BY NUMBERS

| | 2 | 5 | 5 | | | | | | | | |
|---|---|---|---|---|---|---|---|---|---|---|---|
| | 0 | | | | | | | | | | |
| | 0 | 4 | 0 | 0 | 0 | | 3 | 3 | | | |
| 1 | 0 | 0 | 0 | | | | | 3 | | | |
| | 0 | | 0 | | | | | 0 | 8 | 0 | 0 |
| | | 0 | 4 | 3 | 0 | 0 | 0 | 0 | 4 | | |
| 1 | 8 | 9 | 0 | 0 | 0 | | | 0 | 0 | | |
| 7 | | 0 | | 0 | | 3 | 0 | 0 | 0 | 0 | 0 | 0 |
| | | 0 | | 0 | | | | 0 | 0 | | |
| | | | 0 | | | 2 | 0 | 9 | | | |
| | 1 | 0 | 0 | 0 | 0 | 4 | | | | | |
| | 1 | | | | | 2 | 1 | 1 | | | |
| | 8 | 8 | | 1 | 7 | 5 | | | | | |
| | 9 | | 6 | 9 | 0 | | | | | | |

## QUOTE QUEST #8

"Why can't we just climb!"
—John Salathé

---

*Yosemite and Kings Canyon national parks, the U.S.'s third and fourth of fifty-eight, were both created on October 1, 1890.*

# ABOUT THE AUTHOR

Michael Elsohn Ross has guided visitors in Yosemite National Park since 1975 after graduating from U.C. Berkeley with a B.S. in Conservation of Natural Resources. He has worked for Yosemite Institute, the National Park Service, and Yosemite Guides, as well as serving as a field instructor for the Yosemite Outdoor Adventures program with the Yosemite Conservancy for over 30 years. He leads park visitors on walks to learn about wildflowers, birds, bugs, geology, and the general ecology of the Sierra Nevada. Mr. Ross has also been the guide of numerous backcountry trips including journeys for adults as well as families with young children. He is the award-winning author of over 40 books for young people, many of them about bugs and other nature topics. Michael and his family live in El Portal, at the park boundary, in a home over-looking the Merced River and with a view of Chinquapin Fall, the westernmost of Yosemite's hanging valley waterfalls. His website is www.yosemitenaturalist.com

Q. Where can you get answers to hundreds of questions about your favorite national parks?
A. In the National Parks Trivia Series!

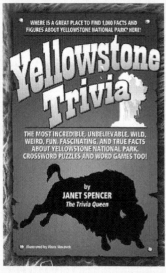

 RIVERBEND PUBLISHING
WWW.RIVERBENDPUBLISHING.COM
PHONE 1-866-787-2363